Ask
George
Anderson

Ask George Anderson

What Souls in the Hereafter Can Teach Us About Life

George Anderson

and Andrew Barone

BERKLEY BOOKS, NEW YORK

THE BERKLEY PUBLISHING GROUP
Published by the Penguin Group
Penguin Group (USA) Inc.
375 Hudson Street, New York, New York 10014, USA
Penguin Group (Canada), 90 Eglinton Avenue East, Suite 700, Toronto, Ontario M4P 2Y3, Canada
(a division of Pearson Penguin Canada Inc.) • Penguin Books Ltd., 80 Strand, London WC2R 0RL,
England • Penguin Group Ireland, 25 St. Stephen's Green, Dublin 2, Ireland (a division of Penguin
Books Ltd.) • Penguin Group (Australia), 250 Camberwell Road, Camberwell, Victoria 3124, Australia
(a division of Pearson Australia Group Pty. Ltd.) • Penguin Books India Pvt. Ltd., 11 Community
Centre, Panchsheel Park, New Delhi—110 017, India • Penguin Group (NZ), 67 Apollo Drive,
Rosedale, Auckland 0632, New Zealand (a division of Pearson New Zealand Ltd.) • Penguin Books
(South Africa) (Pty.) Ltd., 24 Sturdee Avenue, Rosebank, Johannesburg 2196, South Africa

Penguin Books Ltd., Registered Offices: 80 Strand, London WC2R 0RL, England

This book is an original publication of The Berkley Publishing Group.

The publisher does not have any control over and does not assume any
responsibility for author or third-party websites or their content.

PUBLISHING HISTORY
Berkley trade paperback edition / September 2012

Library of Congress Cataloging-in-Publication Data

Anderson, George (George P.)
Ask George Anderson : What Souls in the Hereafter Can Teach Us About Life / by
George Anderson and Andrew Barone.
p. cm.
ISBN 978-0-425-24728-0 (alk. paper)
1. Spiritualism—Miscellanea.   I. Barone, Andrew.   II. Title.
BF1261.2.A53 2012
133.9'1—dc23   2012010590

PRINTED IN THE UNITED STATES OF AMERICA

10   9   8   7   6   5   4   3   2   1

Some of the names and identifying characteristics have been changed to
protect the privacy of the individuals involved.

Penguin is committed to publishing works of quality and integrity.
In that spirit, we are proud to offer this book to our readers;
however, the story, the experiences, and the words are the author's alone.

This book is dedicated to my friend and "son," Terren Graham—I can still hear your laughter in my heart.
—GEORGE ANDERSON

This book is also dedicated with gratitude to Juan Anthony Bidot—your belief in me turned my sky back to blue.
—ANDREW BARONE

ACKNOWLEDGMENTS

For their kindness, for their courage, for their compassion and inspiration, we are profoundly grateful to the following people, both here and hereafter:

Robin Stein and the soul of Morris Stein
Robert Oquendo
Dianne Arcangel
Monsignor Thomas Hartman
Gary Jansen
Pauline and Dennis Patterson and the soul of Jeffrey Patterson
Sharon Friedman
Geri Hashimoto

Joanne Bogenschutz
The Sisters, Servants of Mary
Dr. Raymond Moody
Emily Max and Stanley Oscartu
Rosemary and Luther Smith, and the souls of Drew and Jeremiah Smith
Rebecca Grappo
Denise Silvestro

CONTENTS

The Little Box of Dreams

O ne of my father's favorite expressions was: *Life is always so easy, until somebody comes along, upsets your apple cart, and shows you how hard it really is.* But I believe that none of us wanders so aimlessly through our own lives as to think *any* of it is easy, simply because we haven't yet learned how hard it actually can be. We know instinctively, and quite early on, that in life, some apple carts are destined to be overturned. The longer I live, learn, and grow, the more I realize that quite the opposite of my father's statement is actually the truth. Life is *not* so easy—that is, until someone comes along, helps us pick up our apples, and makes our life easier by illuminating the dark corners of our mind, our heart, and our world. In doing so—in accepting that outstretched hand from sometimes the most unlikely of places—we can learn to live our lives on a clear path of understanding, finding true happiness and enduring peace.

Living and learning on the earth relies on two principles that seem forever linked to our humanity: our need to look *within* ourselves for the skills necessary in order to live, and the need to look *outside* ourselves for the tools necessary in order to survive. Together, they create one of humanity's most powerful life lessons: We need to understand our reason for being, *and* look to others to understand our reason for continuing, in order to flourish on the earth. But something happens to us on our road to understanding—we somehow get lost in our own search, and we struggle needlessly, until we realize that the answers we sought were much closer than we ever realized.

As we walk through the early years of our lives, we tend to view them as a fixed point painted against the backdrop of a movable world—we live in a world we believe is our own making. But circumstances change, and things begin to happen—things beyond our control, and things beyond our understanding. They start to tear at the once-familiar fabric of our existence, separating warp and weft until our own fear and uncertainty render our world completely unrecognizable. But the vagaries of our world and the issues we struggle with are not unfamiliar to everyone—there are those we can learn from, and depend on, to help us understand and mitigate the hard lessons each of us will face in our lifetime. We may eventually learn something from the world we struggle to understand, but we can learn much more from the experiences of others who have navigated this ground before us. Looking forward, toward those who already lived the lesson and earned the prize of knowledge, we begin to discover how important understanding and reassurance can be to our fragile lives. And then hopefully, in time, looking backward from our place of newly found understanding to those we can also help and reassure, we begin to discover the true meaning of our journey on the earth.

How easy it all sounds when we are told. How hard it all is to apply in our own lives, though. We want so much to believe that each of us needs only our own mind and our own hands to face whatever challenges will come our way. But it's also part of the fabric of our humanness to pretend we understand when we don't, and to think we are doing just fine when we aren't. It's a brave but foolish mask we wear, because we somehow feel that admitting we don't have all the answers, or worse—the fact that we *don't even know where to look*—is a sign of weakness or flaw. One of the bravest steps we can take in our lifetime is to *ask* for help from those who have walked the same road, who climbed the same mountain, and who overcame the same obstacles to come to a place of understanding and peace. We can certainly continue blithely, hoping that perhaps by luck or happenstance we may find our way. But trying to endure without understanding exactly where we are on the journey of our lives is to face peril worse than any hard experience we will surely come across. The history of humankind, from the earliest recording, has taught us that those who tried to wander the land alone, who sought to hunt when they had no weapons, or sought to brave the elements when they could build no shelter, not only lived a life of daily imminent danger, but also quickly perished from the earth.

Time may change something different in each of us, but time will certainly wear thin the stubborn veneer of pride in all of us. The hard realization that our lives bear almost no resemblance to the life we had hoped to live, and the difficulty in continuing our once-sure path often begins to trim the prickly edges of our bravado—just enough to admit we don't have all the answers, and we likely may never have them while we are here. It is a moment of clarity greater than any other in our lives when we finally decide that in order to find peace, we first must find answers, accept help, and *learn*. That humble acknowledgment, made at long last by that need to learn, brings us face to face with every human who has ever walked the earth in search of enlightenment, and in pursuit of a better life. Just like in the beginning of time, those whose lives depended on warmth looked to others who knew how to create fire. Those who were hungry looked to others with the ability to hunt for food. And those who pondered the mysteries of the sun, the moon, and the stars beyond them, looked to others with the ability to dream of worlds even greater than their own—to learn that there is a place on a complicated earth under those stars for each of us who struggles for acceptance and understanding. In order to acquire the knowledge, the tools, and the skills we will need to survive, we must depend on the humanity of those who have been on this road before us—in order to learn, to live, and to thrive on the earth.

The search for knowledge is the path to truth, and the search for those who hold knowledge is the path to freedom. The word *teacher* is among the oldest words in recorded language. Its origin can be traced to the Old English *tæcan*, or "one who points out." What is extraordinary about the definition of the word *teacher* is that its original meaning does not include any reference to actually imparting knowledge— only to *point* in the direction of understanding. It is a rather stunning distinction, and a difference well worth noting. The best knowledge we could ever receive is taught by example, and not necessarily by instruction. Teaching by example involves us in our own education in a way that instruction simply cannot. It is a play in which we can see all the characters, notice the width and breadth of the stage, and then watch our drama play itself out before our eyes. We are involved, but only so far as the apron of the stage will let us be—but we can get close enough to the action to see the struggle, feel the tension, and watch the resolution take place. We have lived, if only vicariously, through the experience without actually playing a part, but we have still learned something from it. Through this process, we see the scope of an issue played from beginning to end, we gather valuable tools, and we begin to understand that resolution comes from actually understanding the pitfalls as well as the triumphs. We come to understand that throughout the rest of our lives, the ability to learn from those who have allowed us to watch them play their part has a much more lasting effect than merely being instructed to follow the script, come what may. While valuable from an educational standpoint, in and of itself, *instruction* is merely a set of rules that has no real meaning or clarity to us until we have seen and understood its cause and effect. Without a basic life experience to point to, it seems in comparison only a concept with no actual frame of reference, and then subsequently, no real importance. How often has our human nature gotten the better of us when we see a sign that reads WET PAINT, yet we feel the need to touch it anyway? The sign instructs, but it does not point to the cause and effect of wet paint. If we were learning by example, the practical lesson comes from seeing someone touch the paint and come away with wet fingers. The sign—the *instruction*—is clear, but also fairly meaningless to us, because wet paint looks the same as dry paint. We are told to heed the sign, even though the paint may have dried hours ago. This is the inherent problem with teaching by instruction—it gives us education, but nothing we can take with us on our journey that will have any experiential value. While concepts help us grow in education, they don't always help us grow in knowledge. Part of the learning process in our lives involves seeing through more experienced eyes in our quest to understand for ourselves. We know we may stumble because others have stumbled before us, but we also know we will triumph because we have learned from the triumphs we witnessed. We are assisted in learning just enough so that our own potential fall may not be as far or as hard—we had the arm of someone who knew more than we did on which to steady ourselves. The desire to learn and the willingness to accept help in the learning process are forever bound to each other—it keeps each of us to our purpose of growing and continuing on the earth, and it sheds a light of understanding onto the uncertainty and fear each of us will invariably face as we move forward into untested, uncharted areas of our lives. Help comes to us in many forms, and from many directions, once we are able to acknowledge just how much we need it.

With all of that said, when does the time come that we may consider anyone accomplished enough to go from student to teacher? The answer is both simple and complex. The simple answer is that anything we learn, even as we are still learning, can be passed along to someone else. There will always be someone for whom the experience we just muddled through is fresh and new, and whatever small illumination of our own world we have managed to achieve can be used to cast light on another's darkness of inexperience. This is called "working knowledge"—knowledge that is not quite accomplished, but enough to share with another. We are, each of us, a part of a working-knowledge system that brings information and experience to others, even if we are not quite accomplished ourselves. Working knowledge, however, is an incomplete education—as valuable as it can be to someone just starting out on their journey of understanding, it is still limited by the relative inexperience of those who share it.

The complex answer to the same question requires more introspection, and a willingness to look outside common convention to an area that is frequently the cause of struggle and uncertainty in many of us—our own beliefs. For those limited by what they are willing to allow themselves to believe, the answer may always be complex. But for those whose beliefs have widened enough to permit the possibility that the world is governed by more than that which can be seen with our eyes or felt with our hands, the answer is stunningly simple, and not terribly surprising. No matter how much our understanding of the world may change while we live in it, it will only change so much. And although we will face and overcome many of the struggles and grow from our experiences, we can never really consider our work on the earth finished because of one simple and unequivocal fact— we are still *here*. The people for whom education on the earth is *truly* finished—those who have both fallen and triumphed in every conceivable struggle this world could hurl at them, and who have risen above all of it in order to impart the rare wisdom of life lessons fully learned—are themselves in a very unique and magnificent circumstance: They are ready, willing, and completely able to teach us, because they are no longer on the earth.

I remember as a young boy, coming home from Our Lady of Perpetual Help Catholic school in Lindenhurst, Long Island, and doing what nearly every young Catholic schoolboy does the world over, if he is lucky enough: sitting myself down in front of the one extravagance my parents had in an otherwise frugal and working-class home—a twelve-inch black-and-white Sylvania television set. Television was such a luxury back then that it is so hard to explain to children of this generation, but being able to sit in front of the television in my rumpled school uniform and tie is one of my most vivid memories of childhood. And this, coming from a man who had a rather *vivid* childhood, is saying quite a lot. I remember one day particularly, because it was one of my first real revelations with regard to what it means to be taught life experiences on the earth, and how the education of the teacher so vastly changes everything about the experience they are qualified to teach.

It had already been some time since a bout of chicken pox turned from a mild annoyance to a life-threatening illness when I was six years old. As I started adjusting to a very routine case of simple chicken pox, something unexpected happened. There began a swelling of my brain stem—encephalomyelitis—which alarmed our family doctor so much that he felt it necessary to warn my parents that if my brain continued to swell, life may never be the same for any of us; the illness could leave me with permanent brain damage, irreversible paralysis, or even death. Even in the delirium of the swelling in my brain, I remember so vividly the fear in my parents' faces. They were simple, hardworking people who were ill-equipped to handle the devastation of an illness getting worse by the hour, and could only stand by, panicked and helpless while the doctor fussed and fretted. Although I could not focus on anything in the world outside of my brain, I remember the rosary beads wound so tightly in my mother's hand that they looked as if they threatened to cut off the circulation to her bone-white, clenched fingers.

It was not long after that terrible episode when the television made its first appearance in the living room. To my father, it was a sign of victory—by the grace of God, his family escaped tragedy and was spared his youngest son, and it was also a kind of salve for the rest of the family, who endured such a frightening time and a long, arduous recovery. During my struggle with encephalomyelitis, I lost use of my legs, and even a few months into my recovery I was still crawling. My biggest incentive to crawl out from my bedroom, aside from meat loaf sandwiches my mother would make me, was to see the television in all its splendor, and to watch the images that flickered across that wonderful black screen. To me, it was a little box of dreams—a portal to a world of imagination. Months after the illness, which slightly damaged my brain, I began seeing and hearing the souls of those who had passed to the hereafter, and to me, it was no different than seeing images on a box in the living room— with the exception that the images the souls projected were inside my mind.

The souls appeared to me as if on television, and they spoke to me as if they were telling a story, just like those that emanated from the television. To me, they were a kind of television inside my head, and often just as entertaining. There were grandparents who appeared with the frequency of a situation comedy, and assorted characters I knew from

Catholic school, like St. Catherine and St. Anthony, who seemed to appear as guest stars in the program of my mind. Others, like the woman in lilac-colored robes who visited and spoke often, became as clear and familiar to me as a regular guest on *The Garry Moore Show*. They were as real and as captivating to me as the moving images I saw on the television set. I told my parents about these visits, and although it initially alarmed them, in the end they resigned themselves to the notion that either the brain damage was worse than they originally thought, or that I was having hallucinations, or quite possibly, based on the information I could tell them about relatives who had passed on who frequently visited me, that perhaps there was more to this than they ever wanted to imagine or even dared to think about.

Within a year, however, seeing and hearing the souls had become a matter of fact in my life, and rather begrudgingly, in my parents' lives as well. They seemed resigned to the fact that there was something not quite normal about me, but they still had an innate curiosity about the visitations from people whose lives they remembered, and the messages that often stunned them. While it was then just an odd footnote to my childhood, I still went on with my young life and tried to heed my parents' advice about speaking only at home about what I saw and heard. I had recovered the use of my legs, so there was very little to distinguish me from any other little boy who ran home, found a glass of milk and a sandwich, and sat in front of the magical television set.

My moment of clarity about the souls came at one of the

oddest times in my life, and directly because of the miracle of television. I remember watching an all-time favorite of mine—Jackie Gleason in *The Honeymooners*—and enjoying the episode where Mr. Gleason's character, Ralph Kramden, has an appearance as a game show contestant. The dialogue, from what I remember, was very simple:

"So, Mr. Kramden, where do you live?"
"In Brooklyn."
"Have you lived in Brooklyn all your life, sir?"
"Not yet." (audience laughs)

What seemed like a pretty innocuous joke somehow threw a light switch in my head, and from that point, and onward, what the souls were talking about, and why, made perfect sense. We can, none of us, consider ourselves complete as human beings on the earth—until we have actually *left* it. Until then, we are just as unfinished as a child just taking its first steps in a new world, albeit with perhaps some more life experiences with which to steady ourselves. But the point is this: As much as we can teach each other about the limited experiences we have already gone through, we cannot actually consider ourselves teachers of the human experience until we have completed the cycle of life on the earth, and then see it with a new set of eyes, from a world where we can see each of those experiences in 360 degrees—to understand why they happen, why they are necessary, and how we can come to our own understanding of them. Until then, anything we learn on the earth can only be seen through our limited perspective as human beings in a world we can't fully see. *Yet.* The souls can be considered teachers in the *actual* sense of the word. Not only teachers who can teach by example, but those who can also *point to understanding,* having lived, struggled, and survived the very challenges we face every day. This small yet profound revelation had an impact on my life that has colored every thought process I now have about the value of seeing the issues we face in many more facets than the one directly in front of us. We apparently miss many sides of the same experience because we are not far enough away from them to actually assess their meaning, their scale, and their impact on our lives.

The part of this answer that may be difficult for some to accept, and why I consider it the "complex" answer, is that it requires a belief in the existence of life after this one. But I am a firm believer in the fact that those who are willing to have an open mind and an open heart will look to whatever resource is available for help in dealing with the important issues each of us will face—even if it means stretching their emotional and intellectual boundaries a little. It is for this reason alone that we determined that writing another book, which hopes to answer questions many of us struggle with by looking to the only true teachers—those who have *been here and back*—was important enough to undertake. In many ways, people feel as if their avenues to understanding have been exhausted by the same platitudes, the same rhetoric, and the same clichés that seem to swirl around us in a perfect circle, never actually touching us in a real and personal way. It may be good advice, but it may not be *complete* advice. It does seem to me, however, that after someone has experienced a big enough or damaging enough circumstance that leaves them scrambling for answers—whether through personal loss, financial loss, violence or turmoil—then those rigid walls of who exactly we will and won't look to for guidance seem to waver a bit. Somehow, the more compelling our circumstance, the more willing we are to smash down the walls of disbelief or *nonbelief* to allow for the possibility that we may learn from a source we previously would have scoffed at. Disaster makes humble children of us all. There is no shame in admitting we need help, and when we need help, there should be no stone left unturned in our search for meaning and understanding.

Those who are familiar with my work know I am a medium, which means I have the ability to hear and see the souls who have passed from this lifetime to the next. I have been hearing from the souls just a bit over fifty years, and I have been working professionally as a medium for forty of those years. I believe that it is only through an anomaly in my brain, perhaps as a result of the damage it sustained when I was six years old, that the souls can "speak" to me on a wavelength my brain can understand, very much like the airwaves sent by television transmission to a little box in my living room. I have become so familiar with the souls over the last half-century of hearing from them that we have developed a kind of shorthand language of our own. But the

souls have no specific interest in speaking to me, per se—
they come to speak *through* me to their loved ones. They
speak for many reasons: to provide assurance that they do,
in fact, continue; that they are still involved in our day-to-day
lives; and most important, to help us to continue on the journey that they understand the meaning and value of, even if
we don't quite yet understand. The souls communicate when
we have good times, and they communicate when we find
ourselves in tough times. They continue talking to the earth
as a means of teaching all of us that our lives are a journey,
and each experience we live through and grow past is another
brick in the road that takes us to a world of peace and understanding. The souls understand, because they lived through
every second of the problems each of us face in our daily
lives. But more important, they now understand the *value* of
having had the experience, and having lived through it. This
is where their thoughts on our circumstances and experiences are their most dramatic. They can see the reason and
purpose in everything—good and bad—that happens to
each of us.

All of this is an easy concept for me to understand and take
to heart, because my belief system allows for the fact that
there *are* souls in the hereafter, they *can* speak, and they *are*
willing to help those of us still on the earth. For others, however, it may require a reorganization of thoughts, emotions,
and previously held beliefs to allow for the possibility that
there may be information valuable to us that we might have to
retool ourselves personally and spiritually to accommodate.

It's hard to hand over the reins of our personal beliefs and ideas to something we may or may not believe in, but this book seeks to make no argument for belief in anything but finding the help we need from those whom I believe can help, due to their rather unique perspective. They are the souls—those who have lived on the earth, struggled through the same difficulties we face, and came out the other side of their life experiences with a completely new and fresh understanding of the world they survived—and an understanding of how important, valuable, and *necessary* our life experiences are, even if we can't see any possible value in the difficult circumstances we will all face.

In my work as a medium, the one thing I can always count on is questions from those who come to see me—those who struggle to understand everyday issues that weigh on them and remain pervasive and burdensome in their journey here. They come for answers. The one thing I can always count on when I listen to the souls is getting the answers to those questions. They come with answers borne of the experience of a lifetime of struggle, but a fresh and often surprisingly pragmatic perspective. Their answers reflect a clarity of vision that is hard to argue with, regardless of your beliefs, or lack thereof. I have had many a skeptic come to a session only to be completely entranced by the simplicity of the messages from souls who no longer have any fear or doubt. It is amazing, even to the souls, how many circumstances of the earth, devoid of fear and doubt, can be crystalline and quite dazzling. When they look back at the earth, after having struggled through it and understanding how perilous and frightful the journey can sometimes be, they have a statement that to my dying day I will always be amazed and confounded by. They tell us, *It was all so beautiful.*

Simple and pragmatic answers aside, it is still my belief that the souls are the only real *experts* when it comes to the often difficult experiences we will endure, which are woven into the fabric of everyone's life on the earth. Their advice to the world they are now free from, yet still consider themselves a part of, is sometimes so clear and practical that I often wonder why we cannot see it for ourselves. Maybe it has something to do with our state of mind or the state of our heart when we face challenges. Perhaps if we are able to look at the challenges through a prism of joy, peace, and understanding, just like the souls, the answers really are that clear and simple. Maybe in a world free of fear and uncertainty, it really *can* be beautiful even when it is difficult. We have no way of knowing that. *Yet.* So we rely on those who we can consider to be the ones who truly know and *truly* understand the workings of life on the earth, until we can begin learning from their sage advice and begin the process of inching our own perspective a little closer to theirs. Perhaps we can use the light and air by which they send their simple yet profound messages to lift some of the burdens in our own lives, so that we can also experience some of the dazzling fragments of light from that prism of joy, peace, and understanding while we are still here. This is not only my hope, but the hope of every soul who has ever communicated to those on the earth willing to hear, and *listen* to them.

This book is intended to be simple. It is a simple book of advice. We did not write this book to *instruct* anyone on how to be happy or to find peace—but rather, to allow the souls to *point to understanding*. The quality and the veracity of the source of the advice is for *you* to decide. It is as easy to understand as any advice from those who have completed the wheel of life, and who can comment with absolute certainty and clarity about their existence and ours. Or, it could be as complex as a complete departure from previously held ideological beliefs—if there were any to begin with—affording us a new way of thinking about our world as a tiny fraction of a vast universe, to be judged by us only on the merits of how the words ring in our heart. For those whose belief system will allow, this is a book of questions that encompass many common pitfalls in the human condition, and advice from those who have lived through it, won a hard battle of understanding, and now see these issues in a clear and uncomplicated way—free of the emotion, fear, frustration, and hopelessness that seem to cloud our thoughts and emotions about the problems we face. For those who still struggle with the concept that there are souls around to help us, or that there is a world much more beautiful than our own, I offer this advice: Read the book with an open mind and an open heart. The questions are real—sent to us from all over the world, from people in nearly every corner of the earth who struggle to find peace and some happiness. Perhaps some insight will come from seeing the words in print—people who have laid bare their fear, their pain, their confusion, and their struggle to find hope. Perhaps you will find yourself in one of the questions, you will find some measure of help in one of the answers, where and when the information strikes a chord of truth within you. Perhaps this is the beginning of a new page in your own life and spirituality, having fallen to a place of an unfamiliar lack of direction, and finding that nothing in your field of understanding seems to make sense anymore. If you are on the ground, emotionally, physically, or spiritually, I can tell you with absolute certainty that you are in very good company.

Sometimes we need to have a spectacular fall, or to be laid low by a humbling twist of fate, in order to be able to look upward to things we may not quite have been able to see before. People tend to find their spirituality at the very point when they are closest to the bottom. It is no matter— the easiest way to see all the stars in the sky is to do so with our back to the ground. It's the lowest point we can find— someplace from where we can fall no farther, and still be able to see everything magnificent above us with a view completely unobstructed by our own physical presence.

Since the dawn of time, living and learning on the earth has been made possible by two conventions that seem forever linked to our humanity: our need to look within ourselves for the skills necessary in order to live, and the need to look *outside* ourselves for the tools necessary in order to survive. But we need to learn from those we can trust and count on for knowledge, guidance, and direction. This marriage of our human need to understand, and to be understood by the world around us, is enduring, and will continue regardless of our ability to immediately recognize the source, and despite the confines of time, space, and physical matter. It endures, because the need to be heard and the need to learn, to know, and to understand will always endure. One of us will always be leaning forward, arm outstretched, reaching from a place of uncertainty and need, while another's arm will always be reaching backward, offering us the warm, secure grasp of understanding and peace. I hope you will allow yourself to cling to that miracle of hope, from wherever, and by whomever, it has been extended.

CHAPTER ONE

The Souls and Their World

Dear George Anderson:

Does Heaven actually exist?

—John

The place that has so many names, depending on your religious affiliation or spiritual belief, is the world hereafter—a place where each of us will go after we have lived and worked on the earth. The souls have explained that each of us is on a spiritual journey while we are on the earth, and we are set upon with many struggles, lessons, and circumstances that will test our humanity, our compassion, our ability to love, and our willingness to make the world we live in a better place. How well we have brought these ideals to the earth creates the kind of world we build for ourselves in the hereafter, and how poorly we may have handled what was expected of us creates the circumstances in which we will continue learning and growing in the hereafter, once our time on the earth is done.

In my years of hearing from the souls, I have never actually heard the souls call the hereafter "Heaven." The souls live in a world that is inclusive and respectful of all religious and spiritual beliefs, and they want to make this world as easy to understand as is possible for all of us. The souls simply call their world "the other side." In its simplicity, this phrase bespeaks an interesting dynamic at work. Calling their world "the other side" helps us understand that it is the other, more beautiful side of the world we know and recognize. The souls want us to realize that, but for the troubles that plague the earth, their world is actually what our world *could* be—if we were only able to bring the love, joy, peace, and happiness of their world to ours.

Their hope in explaining their world to us in these practical terms is that we can come to understand exactly why we are *here*. They want us to know that whatever we live through on the earth is part of a well-planned series of events designed to teach us a specific lesson in order to advance ourselves spiritually, so that we may earn the right to move closer to complete spiritual understanding and peace, in a beautiful world that is the reward for having lived here.

I like the phrase "the other side" because it illustrates that there is a second chapter to the story of our lives to which we can look forward, and that no matter how tough things on the earth may become for us, there will always be a happy ending to the story of our lives.

Although the world of the souls often defies a description we can comprehend, given our limited understanding, it is a world that runs parallel to our own. From far away, it looks to be almost a mirror image of the earth, but is generated by the energy of love, peace, and joy, which makes all things come to life. Our worlds are separated only by a thin veil of consciousness—a portal through which the souls can continue to visit the earth in order to help us to help ourselves while we struggle here, and to give us brief, shining glimpses into their world whenever the earth seems to be sagging under the weight of frustration and hopelessness. Our worlds may be very close in proximity, but in terms of spiritual growth and understanding, we will forever be a universe apart, until it is our own time to see their world. It is a place of reward for those who have worked hard to hang on to their humanity, compassion, and love, despite having endured difficult circumstances here, and it is also a place that affords each of us who have failed in our work here an opportunity to fix what we have broken, to repair what we have torn down, and to work on ourselves in a much more forgiving environment, in order to truly earn the peace, joy, and love that await each of us when our life lessons are finished.

The world hereafter also is a place where we come to complete and total understanding. There, we receive the answers to so many of the imponderable questions we have had on the earth about ourselves and the world around us. Questions that haunt us on the earth—like why we live in a world of violence, of hatred, of illness and disease, of discouragement and despair—are answered in detail. Whatever we believed had no hope of explanation in our own world becomes clear and understandable once we leave it. The secrets of the universe are given to us, because we are now at the point where we can understand them fully. All things come full circle in our understanding of so many issues that were so hard to navigate on the earth—relationships, past hurts, disappointments, and failings. We learn why the earth was sometimes so difficult, and we learn how valuable each of those difficult times was, and how they were so vitally important to our spiritual growth.

Many of the souls who have communicated about their world call it a *vacation*—a rest after the earth has worn them down with the difficult issues and circumstances they faced in their time here. Many other souls have called it the reward for having lived on the earth, where problems are pervasive, yet we try to persevere. Regardless of the reason we finish on the earth, the world hereafter is the next chapter in our growth as souls. It is also our prize for having done so much to earn it when we were here. For those who worked hard on the earth, it is a place of rest. For those who struggled with turmoil, it is a place of peace. And for each of us who become frustrated in our attempts to try to live a life the souls themselves would be proud of, the world hereafter is a place of joy.

Dear George:

What do the souls look like? Will we be able to recognize our loved ones when we see them again, or have they changed into some sort of invisible being?

—Anthony

Even though the souls no longer have a need for their physical body, there are attributes and physical characteristics that make each of us who we are. Those things seem indelible, and they remain with us, even when the physical body has long since been discarded.

When I see the souls in a session, they appear almost to be a physical person, but in a hologram state—meaning that I can see the makeup of physical characteristics they have, but they are also at once three-dimensional and nondimensional. They seem to have no actual physical weight, but they have a presence that is strong.

The souls themselves have told me that since their beings are pure energy, they can represent themselves to us in a way we will understand and recognize. How the souls represent themselves seems to do a lot with how they need us to recognize them, and they appear in this way not just for me, but for loved ones who have been lucky enough to receive a visitation from the souls. In sessions, I see the souls rather like a Polaroid photo—they start in almost a white state, and then begin filling in details and recognizable elements a little at a time, so that I can determine whether the soul is male or female, young or old, tall or short. The degree and density to which the souls will appear to me seems more about what they need me to understand in order to get their point across. Some souls stay in a rather translucent state, while others will appear so clearly that I can, for instance, read the numbers on a football jersey one soul had depicted himself in. But all in all, because the souls are pure energy, how they decide to represent themselves depends on what they need us to see, and how strongly they need to project their image for us in order to recognize them.

When people have reported seeing loved ones in spirit, many have remarked that although the souls retained all the physical details they had on the earth, there is something *better* about them—they seem younger, happier, stronger, and more energetic. What becomes remarkable about the souls' appearance is that they become perfect versions of themselves. There is no more illness or infirmity, and no physical problems that may have plagued them on the earth.

In a session I did for a father who had lost his daughter at the young age of twenty-two, he asked me repeatedly what I saw. Throughout the session, I confirmed that the soul was indeed female, young, and calling out to the gentleman in front of me as "Dad," but he kept interrupting to ask me what his daughter looked like. Sometimes I see the souls as a concept—female or male, young or old, etc.—without taking note of their specific physical characteristics, but since this father asked repeatedly, I had to focus in and hope the soul would appear in a more physical way so that I could answer his question. I have to admit, I wondered why the man was so insistent in his request. I thought, *This man knows this soul is his daughter; why does he need me to describe her physical being to him?* But just as I started to think that statement, his daughter did appear strongly enough to see a lovely girl with long, chestnut hair and large green eyes. The souls usually don't portray themselves so precisely for *my* benefit, because I don't know them. But it seemed important to this soul to show me in very vivid detail what she looked like. As I started to explain to the father what I saw, he collapsed into tears, but then smiled and said, "Thank you." I didn't understand until the session started to progress that this man's daughter was trapped in a car that was hit broadside by another vehicle, and the car burst into flames, burning his daughter over nearly her entire body. Her hair, eyes, facial features, and fingers had disintegrated in the fire, and although she survived six weeks in the hospital, infection ended her life. All this brave man wanted to know was whether his daughter was still burned in the hereafter, or if she had returned to the way she looked before the crash, which she plainly and clearly showed us.

I think it helps each of us to understand how meaningful the word "perfect" is when we think of the souls returning to a perfect state when they return to the hereafter. Over the course of a lifetime, things may happen to our physical body, but no matter what does happen, our souls remain perfect, and we continue on in a perfect state when we enter the hereafter.

The souls retain everything physically that is unique and special to them, because how they look on the outside is often a reflection of how they are on the inside, in their soul. It is just a better, more beautiful version that comes to us when we enter the hereafter, much like a caterpillar that sheds its cocoon and becomes a butterfly. The very best of our physicality becomes an imprint on our soul, which we carry with us into the hereafter.

Dear George:

What is the hereafter like? It seems that there are so many conflicting accounts by those who claim to have seen it. What can you tell me about the actual place the souls live?

—Allison

When people ask me to explain the world hereafter, I generally ask them if they want the day pass or the month-long voucher. I think it would be impossible to write down everything the souls have told me about the world hereafter over the last forty years, so I'll do my best to give you the highlights of their world, hopefully in a way that is enough to bring some comfort to you, yet not too long as to flood your head.

When the souls ask us to imagine their world, they ask us to pull a memory from our own minds of the world we live in on one of the best days of our lives. Our physical surroundings may not have changed at all, but suddenly everything looks wonderful because we are filled with joy. This is very much how the souls see their world. Their world is perfect—from the sky, to the sun, to the climate, to the feeling of peace and love that permeates everything and everyone there.

Based on what the souls have told me about their world, I have to conclude that there are many facets to the world hereafter. To them, after they have made the transition, they seem instinctively to understand that their world looks very much like the one they just left—they see things and places that are recognizable, like trees, parks, homes, and lakes—but that the energy of everything around them is so vastly different. They feel the energy of joy and love in everything they touch, everything they see and in everybody they meet. So while the world is completely familiar to them, in many cases, the absolute joy and peace is not—that part is a completely new and wonderful experience.

The souls live in communities, have friends and loved ones, they work in jobs that bring them a feeling of joy and accomplishment, and they enjoy living in a world that has no pain, no violence, no anger, and no regret. Their sky is always clear and sunny, and their sense of well-being is like nothing they had ever experienced on the earth. Many souls have told me they rekindled friendships with people they lost on the earth, and they want to continue working to bring joy and peace to others, especially their loved ones who are still here.

One of the more fascinating things that the souls have told me about their world is that it is a world of their own consciousness. It seems that we "build" our world, according to what we feel we need, until we grow in understanding and we don't feel the need to look at our world in terms of material things anymore. Many have told me that they choose the type of home they want to live in, the type of area that will bring them happiness, and were able to surround themselves with people who bring them love and joy. Our world in the hereafter depends very much on our own imagination, because it is what we longed and hoped for on the earth, and it is created in the way we believe our own world should look. The souls have told me that anything that eluded us on the earth that we found important—money, fancy things, doting friends, a grand place to live—is given to us in abundance in the hereafter. So in the first days, months, and perhaps even years, the world the souls choose to live in is a reflection of everything they didn't have on the earth. They seem absolutely giddy about this one fact of their new life—that they can have anything they ever wanted.

But a funny thing happens to the souls as they grow in knowledge and understanding in the hereafter. They start to realize that it was never *things* that they missed on the earth, and that things don't bring you joy. Helping others, helping those on the earth, and living a life of joy seems to become the only things that actually matter to the souls. And their world begins to reflect that change. Their existence becomes more simple and austere, but their purpose explodes into joy. I think sometimes this is why we can't really say with any complete confidence *exactly* what the souls' world looks like, because it is so vastly different from soul to soul, depending on their desires and needs, but it also changes as the souls change in knowledge and spirituality in the hereafter.

Instead of trying to explain the world hereafter from the point of view of the souls, I mostly rely on my own glimpses into their world, and I can only describe the things I see by comparing them with what I know on the earth.

When I was eleven or twelve years old, a boy in the neighborhood brought over a canister that he kept in a paper bag. It was a gift from his grandfather, and he carried it like a priceless treasure. I begged to see what was in the bag, and after some thought, and promises that I would be extra careful, he pulled the canister from the bag, told me to hold it up to my eye, and twist it around. It was the first time I had ever seen a kaleidoscope.

I pointed the kaleidoscope to the nearest landmark—a tree—and turned the canister just as I was told. I immediately felt the hairs on the back of my neck stand up. As I turned the cylinder, the tree burst into millions of colors, which danced and sparkled as if the tree had come to life. The colors were dazzling and brilliant, and they moved rapidly, almost with the intention of trying to outdo their last amazing display. I was mesmerized by the image of the tree that seemed to move at will and throw millions of lights and colors from its branches in a carefree and graceful way. Although this was the first time I had ever heard of a kaleidoscope, let alone peered through one, there was something so oddly familiar about the sights I saw through that magnificent instrument. The colors, the particles of light that danced, while still resembling a tree, brought me right back to the souls. I had visions of the souls where they came to me on what looked like clouds of millions of tiny lights at their feet, which swirled together and came apart, creating familiar shapes, and then undulating again into another pattern. I also recognized the colors that seem to follow every movement the souls make when they appear to me—the colors created by the movement of their bodies mixed and changed, yet still maintained the appearance of a fully recognizable human body. It came to me quite clearly that day that this is the world of the souls—it is ever changing, filled with light, and imbued with colors that spill forth, change, regroup, and become something else, because they are made up of the energy of love and joy. Their world undulates because the energy is in constant movement, and can only sit still long enough to create a semblance of a physical form that we on the earth would recognize. But to the souls, it is so much more.

I had an occasion to see once again those magnificent images of the world hereafter, much later in life, when during a time of my own struggle, I was visited by St. Anthony, who took me to the world hereafter to help me understand more about the problems I faced at the time. Although his words were comforting, I found myself drawn to the water of the lake he stopped in front of. It shimmered with light and color that seemed to move on its own—first it was water, then it was a billion diamonds that came together to create a kind of water, then dispersed and regrouped with colors and shades I had never seen on the earth. Yet all the time, to me it still looked like water, the trees looked like trees, and the ground looked just as familiar as the ground I walk on the earth, with one exception—they *live*. They are filled with energy and joy to the point where they can no longer be inanimate—they move and swirl in a display of beauty that brings hope and joy to whoever will look at it. Everything in the hereafter, from the ground below, to the sky above, *lives*.

The world hereafter seems to be, at least to the souls who are now lucky enough to live there, a world of endless possibility and beauty, yet still a faint reflection of what our world could be if it were filled with love, peace, and the energy of happiness and goodwill. The souls understand their world now to be *perfect*—a perfect image of what our lives could have been on the earth, but for the problems we have here, and our apparent unwillingness to try to make it any better. There are no more problems in the world hereafter—no one grows old, no one ever becomes sick, and no one ever feels the pain of loneliness or frustration. We may call it *Heaven*, and it is an ideal we can only aspire to, but to the souls who now enjoy a world they earned through their struggles on the earth, at long last, it is called *home*.

Dear George:

What happens when we die? Where do we go, and do we know that we died?

—Bob

I remember many years ago watching the legendary Walter Matthau tell a story on the *Tonight Show Starring Johnny Carson*, in which he recounted working with children on the set of the movie *The Bad News Bears*. During casting auditions for the child actors, he asked routine questions of each of them until he came upon a young girl.

"What does your mommy do?" he asked the girl.

"She's a housewife."

"And what does your daddy do?" he continued.

"He's dead," she answered.

"Well, what did he do before he died?" he asked.

The young girl made a grotesque face, clutched her heart, and fell to the ground to illustrate. The story was met with riotous laughter from the audience, including myself. I marveled at how clear and pragmatic even the most complex of issues are in the mind of a child. Maybe we all need to be a little more childlike in our understanding of just what death is.

Because we understand no other point of view than from our physical perspective, death seems to be a devastating and terrible event—the time at which our physical bodies cease to function. But to the souls who have made the transition out of their physical body and to a world unbound by anything physical, physical death is a very inauspicious start of a lifetime none of us could have ever imagined.

No matter what the cause of our physical death, the souls have said that the transition from one world to another is as easy and uneventful as moving from one room to another in our own homes. No fanfare, no drama, and no fear. In so many instances when the souls have talked about their physical passing, not once has any mentioned fear or reluctance about the actual stepping forward into the world hereafter. At the moment of their physical death, the souls recount seeing a *portal* open before them, where they can feel, see, and understand the world hereafter. They recount that they can immediately feel the peace and love emanating from the portal, and they feel drawn to it like a moth to flame. There seems to be something irresistible about the light and love that pours out to greet them, much like a carpet that is rolled out to their feet, beckoning them to step forward. And they do. It feels right to them, and it feels safe and secure. They know that this is the end of the life they knew on the earth, and the beginning of something spectacular.

Very often the souls have told me that at the moment of

their passing, they see friends, loved ones, and even pets standing on the other side of this portal, welcoming them. To the souls of loved ones who passed before us, this is a moment of great joy and pride. We make the decision to walk forward to this world, because it seems the right thing to do. What has surprised me about some of the stories the souls will tell is that I don't hear any moment of conflict in them, or any talk about a need to look backward at the world they are leaving. I think they must find their new world so strange and beautiful that natural curiosity leads them forward, where they instantly feel the peace and love that resonates from the other side.

Just like the world hereafter is difficult to exactly describe because it is as unique and individual as the soul whose world it now is, so it is the same with our moment of passing. Although the pattern of events stays the same, each passing seems to have something unique, designed to best benefit whoever is now walking through the portal. Some souls who lived and died in a state of turmoil on the earth have recalled finding quiet—a kind of quiet that made their heart still and their peace return. One soul of a young woman who passed from an intended overdose because she suffered from bipolar depression and mania, told me that she felt as if she were enveloped in a velvet blanket, where the dark was so peaceful and easy on her eyes that she felt herself want to sleep. She did not know for how long she slept, but recounted that once she awakened, the sun, the sky, and the world she waked to began very dimly, as if it were the early morning of a new day, and began to brighten as she felt more sure of herself and more comfortable with her surroundings. It was the first of many times I have heard the souls bring up this kind of "sleep state" that seems designed to quiet the noise of a difficult life filled with turmoil, so that the souls can regroup and begin again from a point of peace.

Other souls have told me that the transition was quite unexpected and a bit of a happy surprise. A young man whose parents came to see me after his passing found some comfort in hearing that their son, an expert swimmer who inexplicably drowned off the coast of Long Island, did not suffer prior to his passing, as they feared he would have. Drowning, according to the souls, is one of the easiest and most pleasant ways to pass, because once we understand not to panic, the water becomes warm and comforting, and we drift through our passing. This young man explained that while swimming, he felt his legs begin to cramp, which seemed to set off a chain reaction in both his arms and legs. He felt himself becoming immobilized by both the pain of the cramps and fear, until he felt something or someone tell him to stop moving. He decided to listen to what he heard, and he felt himself floating aimlessly at first, and then in a direction that he could feel. Once he stopped thrashing, he found that the movements of swimming became easier, and he started to swim easily to the shore. As he swam, the water became warmer, clearer, and by his account, more *lovely*. He swam in an easy way to the shore and began to walk out of the water, only to see that it was not at all the shore he had left—

it was beautiful and sunny, and perfect. When he saw his dog, one that had passed over a few years before, he started to understand that something was very different, and he continued up the beach where he began meeting other smiling, happy young people. He began to realize he had passed on, and was amazed at how he couldn't actually pinpoint the time that he'd actually died. It seemed so natural and organic to him. He acknowledged that he was quite surprised, and rather happy, to find himself in the beautiful place he was.

One story of passing has stuck with me for many years, and was both heart wrenching to hear, but helpful to know. I am particularly sensitive to children who must endure any kind of suffering on the earth, perhaps because I was made to suffer at a young age because of my ability. But it's always hard to hear any story, no matter how wonderful the ending, of any child who has to suffer. I understand in my brain that each of us must struggle in some way on the earth in order to continue on in the hereafter, but what my mind understands, my heart is often at odds with. I know that children who suffer on the earth benefit from their suffering in ways that even *they* know were a blessing in disguise. But I am human, and it's sometimes hard to grasp.

The distraught parents of a ten-year-old girl came to see me shortly after her death. When she did not return home from school one day, her parents and the police searched for her until they came upon a grisly scene—the girl, apparently the victim of a sexual assault, had her skull bashed with a rock. They came to me frustrated, angry, and with strong

feelings of guilt and remorse that they were not there to protect their daughter from the depravity of a twenty-one-year-
old man, who was later caught and convicted of her murder.

In the session an extraordinary thing happened—the
young girl spoke about her abduction by her assailant, and
told her parents that her heart was full of fear. "But then the
Lady appeared," she told us. She showed me the image of the
Blessed Mother—the Virgin Mary—who she said came to
her and told her it was time to go. Incredibly, she told us that
once the Lady held her hand and brought her away, she was
no longer scared, and she didn't feel the effects of the brutal
beating. Her little soul left her body before the physical
body was actually dead. The story lingers with me to this
day because I had never heard of the souls being so compassionate and understanding where they would spare the needless suffering of a human being, and decided to remove her
from the earth without having to endure any more fear or
brutality. When we think of the souls and the world hereafter, and their ways to make each of us feel loved, secure, and
peaceful even through the event of our physical death, I
think the story speaks volumes to how carefully and how
fully we are engaged and protected by the souls when it is
our time to pass.

Although there are many different stories and as many
different circumstances of passing as there are stars in the
sky, it seems to be that our passing is custom-made to help
each of us find a way to transition from this lifetime to the
next in the easiest, most comfortable and peaceful way the

souls can manage for us. It helps to know this when we think of those we love who may be nearing the moment of death due to illness, or those whose passing seemed so chaotic and sudden that we would be hard-pressed to consider *anything* about it comforting or peaceful. But it does happen, and the souls make it so—we pass from this world to the next through a portal of comfort and peace, to a world of beauty, imagination, and love that defies anything we could have imagined for ourselves in this lifetime.

Dear George:

There are a variety of books on the subject of Near Death Experiences or NDEs. They seem to run the gamut of experiences from peaceful to frightening and everything in between. Can you tell me why the stories aren't more similar if it is the same place these people have seen? Is there any way to know for sure that what people had was a real NDE?

—Vincent

I think perhaps more than any other glimpse into the world of the souls, none is more powerful or enduring than the phenomenon we know as the Near Death Experience. I am very lucky to have experience with this phenomenon from what the souls have told me, what those who experienced have told me, and what some of the best researchers in the field have come to understand as a real and true experience of touching the world hereafter. As I already mentioned, there is a portal through which the souls can move about on the earth in order to help bring us signs of hope and encouragement. The same portal is our exit door from this world to the next. So it stands to reason that there will be the occasional passing through this portal for reasons that may seem purely accidental, but is actually designed to bring a powerful message from the world hereafter to the earth. In order to understand how and why they happen, we need to go to the experts, the souls, and the very people who have taken a look behind the veil, and have returned to their lives, changed forever by the experience.

Researchers like Dianne Arcangel, Dr. Raymond Moody, and Dr. Elisabeth Kübler-Ross have each chronicled thousands of cases in which people experience a physical death, slip through the portal of transition and into the world hereafter, only to come back through to the earth again. Each researcher, because of their distinct background, has looked at the experiences they feel qualify as an NDE through the lens of the scientific, the spiritual, and the practical, in order to determine if they were bona fide NDEs. The results of their findings have been revolutionary. They have determined that our consciousness does, in fact, continue through time and space, even if our physical bodies do not. The souls have also weighed in, but for a very different reason—to try to explain why NDEs happen, their significance to our world, and why the experience seems to etch itself permanently into the hearts and minds of those who found themselves, even for a brief, shining moment, among the souls and their extraordinary world.

The Near Death Experience usually follows a very predictable pattern—people, through some kind of physical trauma, find themselves in circumstances where their physical bodies are no longer able to sustain life. They begin to experience the process of *dying*—the heart stops beating, and the brain is unable to send any signals to keep the body alive. In those few minutes when the body begins to cease functioning, some people have experienced the sensation of leaving their physical being and traveling away from their circumstance, even as they remain conscious of every detail of where they are and what is happening. The soul pulls away from the physical body and seems to hover awhile at the portal between this world and the next. From this point and onward, the individual stories, though linked by some basic commonality, are as unusual and unique as the people themselves.

In some of the NDEs that were studied, the experience seems to begin in different ways. People have reported going back in time, to when they were children, and they begin living through memories that happened in the past, but with a new and somewhat different perspective. They are conscious of present time, yet they find themselves living in a memory of the past. It is, to them, as if the past, present, and the future are happening all at the same time. Others have reported their NDE beginning with the feeling of unusual peace and serenity, as if the current crisis of dying holds no importance to them. They feel liberated and disconnected from fear and concern, and they discover a curious ability to look into the hearts and minds of those still on the earth—to sense their feelings and to understand their thoughts and emotions. The vast majority of those who have experienced an NDE report being surrounded by light and energy, and feeling themselves drift quickly through a kind of tunnel that is brightly lit in the distance. They find themselves moving at incredible speed, while hearing and seeing images and people from their past. In nearly every one of the cases studied that were found to be real and genuine, those who had passed through the portal into another dimension are fully aware that they are leaving the earth, yet they don't seem to care. They find themselves entranced by the light and warmth, and their emotional well-being becomes so strong that they *want* to continue, because the peace and calm become an irresistible force.

This is where the stories seem to converge: All who have experienced an NDE find themselves at the cusp of the world hereafter, either walking or floating toward that world and the souls who are already there. While they are able to feel the joy, love, and peace of that world, they understand that they are only at the very edge of this world. At this point, however, their thoughts of peace and serenity are interrupted by admonitions that they must return to the earth—that although they find themselves at the cusp of a new world they want so much to enter, they may not enter because it is not their time. Some have reported being told to go back by a kind stranger. Others have reported seeing precious loved ones again who tell them that unfortunately they cannot stay. And then, by drawing a breath of consciousness, they are gone in an instant, and back to the world and the circumstance from which they came.

The field of Near Death Experiences is not where my expertise lies; I only know what I have been told. But I do understand from what I have been told by those who have researched them, those who have lived them, and the souls who have commented about them, that there is nothing more powerful to a human being than being touched by the world hereafter. It changes them in a way that cannot always be understood, but the effects are life-changing nonetheless. Some are grateful for the experience, and want to share the feeling of light and beauty with anyone who will listen. Others find themselves moving through periods of abandonment and depression, feeling that they were rejected by the world they so desperately wanted to stay in. But the most valuable information I have heard seems to come from the souls, who can explain what happens without the emotion of feeling it all over again. Their explanation for NDEs—why they happen, and why they endure—is both unusual and poignant.

The souls tell me that in essence, Near Death Experiences are postcards from another world to the earth. Just as vacation postcards are designed to give us a quick update and glimpse into an exotic place, so are the experiences some will have in the course of their lifetime. The souls rely on those who have had the extraordinary experience of having visited their world to bring the joy and peace of that moment to anyone who will benefit from having heard about it. It's their way of sending reminders to the earth that there is so much more to come, if we can believe, if we can hope, and if we can endure. Those who lived through their NDE become beacons of light and hope on the earth. They are now emissaries of a world of wonderment and beauty, and because they are ordinary people with no reason to complicate their own lives with the reality of such an incredible experience if it did not actually happen, their stories carry a familiar ring of truth to those who want to know and understand.

Unfortunately, not everyone who claims to have an NDE has actually had one. When someone tells me they've had a Near Death Experience I keep in mind what both the experts and the souls have told me and I listen for the familiar buzzwords and landmarks in their account that lend truth to their story. There are some cases where I can tell the person has not experienced an actual NDE. Many make up stories to gain some notoriety or attention. These accounts typically involve fear, grotesque images, visions of terrible places and people, and are heavily steeped in religion. I don't want to be cruel, because some people who feel they have had an actual NDE are very well-meaning, if not slightly misinformed. The souls have also told me that *anything* that happens that involves the souls or the hereafter will be peaceful and comforting. Anything that centers around evil, ill will, fear, unhappiness or discomfort is *not at all* connected to the souls. Those feelings do not exist in the hereafter. And although some people can prove they "died" for a few minutes and had some sort of experience, it does not always qualify as an NDE. Very often, their negative experiences and ugly images and feelings are products of their unconscious mind. It is unfortunate, but it does happen. Though it may seem believable to whoever may have experienced and felt it, it is simply not an experience that involved the souls or the world hereafter.

Another thing I have noticed about Near Death Experiences when they are true and real is the fact that no matter how many times they are told, and no matter how long ago they happened, those who have experienced this remarkable phenomenon never forget even the smallest detail, or feeling, or sense that they originally had the moment the NDE happened. This is also one of the hallmarks of the circumstance that researchers and scientists have become fascinated with—the story simply does not change, not even a little bit. I have often told the story about my own father, who at the age of twenty-one years old was crushed between two railroad cars when he worked on the Pennsylvania Railroad. His experience of leaving the operating table and finding himself running through a beautiful field until he was met by three souls who explained that he must go back, both beguiled and haunted him his entire life. In retelling the story, even after many years, he could not help but choke with emotion when he explained how the three souls in white robes turned to him and said, "George, it's not your time. You must go back. You must go back, George." It was heartbreaking to hear so much emotion in his voice when he said those words, and a part of him always felt slighted that he was not able to stay and enjoy the grace and beauty of that world. So much so, that on his deathbed when he was seventy-eight years old, he summoned enough energy to joke, "Well, now they HAVE to take me." And at last, they did.

Near Death Experiences will always hold a special place in the minds and hearts of those who were graced with a look behind the veil, in order to tell our world how magnificent it will be, if we can only hang on through the often bumpy road we travel. The souls entrust a lucky few with this knowledge, but like anything else, the amazing experience comes with responsibility and sometimes pain. It's painful to come to the well of perfect peace and not be permitted to drink, but the memory of that place keeps a fire burning in the hearts of each of us who witness firsthand or even just hear these incredible stories. One day—in time, and at last—it will be not only our story, but our life.

Dear George:

I had a session with you a few years ago, and one thing that stuck out in my mind was that you repeated the

phrase "I am in a safe and happy place" more than once.
It struck me as odd, knowing what you have said and
written before about the souls and what a peaceful world
they have. Why would they need to point out to us that
they are "happy and safe"? Is there a reason for us to
think otherwise?

—Walter

The souls do and say a lot of things during the session, and I've found that most of the time they repeat themselves because they know we may not hear it unless it is drummed into us over the course of a few mentions. This happens because *we* have issues with a world we cannot yet see, not the souls. In order to keep us from fearing the worst about them, they go out of their way to make assurances to us that their world is everything they say it is, and more.

I notice that the very phrase you mentioned comes up in sessions more than once when there was a violent or unexplained passing. We are not always lucky enough to know the details of our loved one's passing, and sometimes a passing brings with it more questions than there are answers. So the souls try to steer us as best they can from thinking the worst, and they try to beat us to the punch with statements that hopefully are strong and passionate enough to make us understand that they mean what they say.

It is human nature to conjure the worst scenarios when we have no information to go by, rather than to settle into the notion that all is well and most probably will be. I have found myself making plans to go to a sunny spot on vacation, and once I have made careful plans, find myself worrying: What if it rains for four days? What if the flight is canceled? What if I get stranded and can't come back to meet my clients? The bigger question here is: Why do we do it to ourselves? Don't we have enough to worry about?

And so it goes with those who have loved ones in the hereafter, who come to a session convinced that they must know for sure that no harm has come to those who they cannot immediately see or hear from. We feel we must know for sure that our loved ones are in the kind of beautiful world they deserve to be in, and in so many cases it falls to the souls to try to help each of us understand a little more about their world, in order to keep us from worrying after them. I find this particularly funny because the souls, in a world of beauty, are perhaps the *last* people we should worry about. They are doing better than we could ever imagine for them. But they understand that our world is full of misunderstanding, uncertainty, and fear, so they have to speak on our level to help us understand a little better about their world. They do this for us—not for themselves—because they know how much it matters to us.

Concern about this issue usually comes from parents who have lost a child, or from those who had a loved one who was abused emotionally or physically by someone who had also subsequently passed. The first group is very understandable—parents, no matter where they are, worry after their children and want to know for certain that they are happy, well loved and well cared for. It's a very human concern, and one that the souls try to address very straightforwardly. So they tell us repeatedly that the children are "safe and happy," and then go on to explain just who is caring for them. I can't tell you how many hearts that simple statement has eased. So the souls will say it over and over until we understand, or at least until they wear down the fears we may have. It's just part of the souls' assurances to us that all is well and they are in a position of love and care even better than a parent could hope for.

Another more difficult reason the souls feel the need to assure us that they are "safe and happy" is when there is an incidence where both the victim of abuse and the tormentor pass together, as in cases of murder-suicide. This is a real concern for many people, but they should not be troubled. In a world like ours, things like murder and suicide happen— they are part of the human condition. However, in a place like the hereafter, people who have made mistakes or did terrible things here come to understand their failings, and try to rebuild their lives and atone for the mistakes they have made. How the hereafter works its magic on situations like these comes to actually teach us a thing or two about forgiveness and understanding. One of the things people find hardest to understand about the souls who encountered violence or abuse on the earth is that they are completely surrounded by love in the hereafter. Nothing of the violence they experienced on the earth can ever touch them again, because it literally doesn't exist in the hereafter. They understand it and they live it now—but the hard part is trying to help us understand in a way that will make sense to us, that they are very happy, very safe, and continuing with their lives, for the better, in the hereafter. The souls never want us to worry after them, because it is a profound waste of our time and energy. They are doing better than we ever could have hoped, and living in a peace and joy we can only dream about.

Dear George:

Why do the souls continue to talk? Aren't they finished? Why would they spend a second longer than they had to here if their world is so much better than ours?

—Allan

There are quite a few souls who have communicated to me that they would never return to the earth—that the world here was too difficult, and it was fraught with too many problems. From the peace and safety of their world now, they will only come so close—just close enough to be heard, but not close enough to involve themselves in the emotion, the struggle, and the ongoing matters of the relentless world we live in. There are, however, many other souls, who, in looking at their own lives as a series of ups and downs, want to share what they've learned as a result of having lived an entire life on the earth. Their hope is to make the road a little easier for whoever will listen and take their words to heart.

There is something within many of us that wants to teach what we know—to help others avoid the problems we faced, and perhaps spare them some of the frustration and disappointment that seems to go with any difficult journey. The souls are no different in that regard. It also seems that part of some souls' spiritual growth in the hereafter includes helping us on the earth to avoid the very same issues that seemed to cloud their learning and development on the earth.

There was a young man who came through in a session who passed on as a result of gang violence. Although it was still a bit of a struggle for him to admit he contributed in a large way to his own passing, he did concede that he made poor choices, motivated by greed and a desire to feel important around those he thought were his friends. Part of his soul growth in the hereafter, he explained, was to try to be a kind of guardian angel to his two younger brothers who appeared to be drifting down the same path on the earth. His hope, like many of the souls who find it important to share what they know with the earth, was to share his knowledge and perhaps help another young person to avoid the same mistakes—and perhaps the same fate.

Another interesting reason the souls continue to communicate to the earth is that they want to shatter the myth that everything ends in death. They want to help each of us understand that the life we see is only a small fraction of the life we live. Life continues, just as we do. So they speak to their loved ones, they speak to people like me, and they speak to whoever will listen with their heart. Having seen our world from the perspective of their new life of peace, it's much easier to see the places where we will get caught up or trapped by bad choices. If anything, the souls' words to the earth are mile markers on our individual roads; they can instruct, they can warn, and they can steer us away from potentially dangerous curves and surprise turns in our own road. The souls know they can't force us to listen or take their advice, but they know they can inspire us, and perhaps provide some strength when we feel our resolve sagging.

Yes, the world of the souls is much better than our own, and yes, the souls are very much finished physically with this world. But the desire to be a source of hope and to really make a difference in the lives of others seems as important to the souls as the air we breathe is to us. The souls have never stopped talking to the earth, and their communications come in many different forms. Sometimes they come in the form of words that appear in dreams or visitations. Sometimes they come in the form of signs, which on the surface seem random or coincidental, but point to a specific circumstance we need to think about. And sometimes, they come in the form of somebody else on the earth being shepherded into our lives, someone who can really make a difference in the way we think or live. The souls are very good at creating the opportunities through which others on the earth can find and help us. They do what they know they need to in order to keep us to our path, keep us walking toward our goals, and also keep the fire of hope alive within us. It may be their generosity, or it may be a part of their own continuing soul growth, but at the end of the day, they just want to make the road a little easier for the next person who wanders through. I've seen their wise words and carefully chosen signs change the lives of people here for the better. And for that, I know I and many others will always be grateful to them.

Dear George:

You stated in an interview once that there are lower levels in the afterlife and that people who do wrong to others will hold themselves there and learn. How can we be sure that when we connect with the afterlife that the souls from the lower levels are not contacting us? I don't wish to sound fearful, as I actually have never experienced anything negative. I guess if we have negative on earth then we must have negative of some kind in the afterlife. I have heard others talk of this and just wanted some clarification.

—Debra

There is no negativity whatsoever in the world hereafter. I don't think I can say that statement enough times in my life, or at least enough to make people understand and take it to heart. But the souls have told me consistently and candidly that the world hereafter is a world of peace, joy, and light—no negativity can live there.

There are souls for whom the journey on earth was a difficult and unhappy one. They may have veered off their chosen path and into a world of violence, destruction, and turmoil for themselves and others whose paths crossed theirs. When they pass on to the hereafter, and enter a world of peace and joy, they come to find, perhaps for the first time in their lives, that nearly everything they had done on the earth was a waste of time and energy. Perhaps even worse—that they caused pain, hardship, and even death to another soul on their journey.

In the hereafter, as part of a world of understanding and compassion, we are not judged—but we do judge ourselves. We look at the life we lived on earth, and we understand the damage and hurt we may have caused. Those who have entered the world hereafter and have found the peace and joy they yearned for all their lives understand that perhaps they have not yet earned it, so they voluntarily pull themselves away from the Infinite Light—the source of all peace and joy—until they feel they have earned the right to move forward in peace. No matter how long it takes, the opportunity to continue learning and growing, and making up for our previous existence is always there for us. Now, in a world of joy, these souls understand the value of compassion and understanding, and work very hard to earn the joy and peace they now live surrounded by.

Levels is a word that has been misused so many times, with regard to the souls and their world. Firstly, let me tell you that *all* the souls can communicate from the other side if they choose to, and many have—even those who have done terrible things on the earth, if only to apologize and try to make amends as part of their spiritual healing and their desire to fix what they had broken on the earth. The levels some souls place themselves in are not so much like floors of a building, where souls are separated, but rather like grades, as in school. The souls are all in the same place, but not in the same "grade." Some more advanced spiritual souls could be considered like PhDs, while other souls who struggled with their journey in their lifetimes may be at a first-grade level. If you think of the hereafter as a party, you would know that you would find many different people, from all walks of life and education levels at that party. It is very much the same for the souls. They are on different "levels" but all in the same place, and all have the opportunity to advance in the community of souls, and continue their spiritual growth. No one is ever forgotten or cast aside in the world hereafter, and each of us has the opportunity to continue learning and growing in an atmosphere of peace.

Dear George:

Are animal souls just as important as human souls? Are they not the same when it comes to God? Why do I always hear that their souls go to a different place, like they are different? I know I would want to go where they are.

—Marion

I can tell you without reservation that animal souls are just as important as their human counterparts, and perhaps a little more so. I don't know why some religions insist on portraying animals as somehow less important in their journey on the earth. Many animals live a courageous life after being mistreated, abused, and even tortured, without being able to ask for help. They are the silent victims of cruelty at the hands of people here who have no respect, understanding or love for those who have been sent to the earth to teach us patience and understanding. The souls have called animals the "eyes of God" on the earth because they see without judgment, love without condition, and give without expectation. That is the perfect image of the Infinite Light. According to the souls, cruelty to an animal is considered a worse offense than cruelty to another human being because animals are at the mercy of those who they love, even when they are abused and mistreated. Conversely, kindness and compassion to an animal is considered one of the greatest achievements in our soul growth on the earth, because it shows that we understand and value the example of the Infinite Light that has been brought to the earth. So yes, all our beloved animals will be in the hereafter waiting for us when our journey here is finished, and they also find a life of reward for their own journey on the earth.

Dear George:

What do the souls consider the most important thing they've learned since moving on to the hereafter?

—Margaret

There are so many things the souls have told me about their world that I would be hard-pressed to think of just one benefit they find once they have passed on. But I can name many that the souls feel are among the most important things they have found about their new world that made their transition worth every second of pain or struggle they may have endured to reach it.

One of the things the souls seem the most happy about is the fact that once they move on to the hereafter the troubles of the earth disappear for them. Many people on the earth live in pain—emotional, physical, even spiritual pain. Some-times they are the product of badly planned lives, tragic cir-cumstances, addictions, frustration, unhappiness, or an inability to love themselves or others. So many people func-tion while hiding their pain from even those who most care about them—they wander through their lives not hoping for much and expecting even less. I find this to be one of the most profound tragedies of the earth—that people move around silently in their pain without ever once asking for help. On the other side, however, there is a rebirth that hap-pens to these people. They discover, perhaps for the first time, what it feels like to be held in high regard, to be cared about, and to be loved. Many souls have expressed to me that it was as if a light went on and they could finally see their lives and what they could be. They find the kind of peace and joy they were searching for, and it has made a dif-ference in everything about them. During sessions, I can actually feel and hear joy emanating from them, and they are proud to be able to tell people how much life has changed for them—for the better.

Another thing that seems to be of great importance to the souls is the fact that anything that eluded them on the earth is found in abundance in the hereafter. Many people go without on the earth—sometimes it is food, or friendship, love or family, or finding simple kindness. These souls go to the hereafter and find the things they longed for every day of their earthly lives, laid out for them in unending amounts, for which they are so grateful.

I used to joke with people when my mother was alive that I'll be doomed when she does actually pass, because then I'd have no way of pretending I wasn't home when she "called."

My mother had a difficult life as a child, and the effect of it continued into her adulthood and almost completely through her life. She grew up Eleanor Brogden in Harlem, New York City, during a time when the country was reeling from the Great Depression. Nowhere were the effects felt greater than in her household of two older sisters and a younger brother, dealing with the recent death of their father, and trying to care for their mother, who had asthmatic episodes so debilitating that she often had to be hospitalized. During the times that their mother was hospitalized, the children did their best to forage for food from neighbors, and did the best they could to care for themselves, with only the occasional looking-in of neighbors. My mother and her siblings often came home to a bare icebox with nothing to eat, and they frequently went to bed hungry, until one day during the Christmas holiday when their mother was once again hospitalized, they were rounded up by the Child Welfare Agency and brought to different orphanages around the city. It would be a fair statement to say that the effects of a childhood mired by hunger, fear, and instability haunted my mother throughout her life, even though she did marry, raise a family, and stayed devoted to her Catholic faith. But there was a depression and anxiety that was pervasive in her life, and although she considered herself content, I would not have considered her happy.

The things that always amazed me about my mother were her devotion to faith, and her unshakeable belief in me. She never wavered in her belief that the souls communicate to me, and although sometimes her adulation was embarrassing, it was still nice to know she was certain the souls chose me to communicate for them because I was meant to teach people hope. One of my more poignant memories of her came literally the day she passed on. She had the nurse place a call to me, in effect, to ask permission to go. She was so ill and had lingered so long in illness that I was incredulous that she would even consider hanging around a second longer than she had to. She simply asked if it was okay to go, and I told her, "God has given you a passport—take it. Daddy needs you more than we do." And with that, she took her place in a beautiful world, with plenty of things to eat, loved ones to care for her and to care about, and the stability of a constant and dependable new life.

As I said, I was afraid that I would not stop hearing from my mother when she entered the hereafter, but a curious thing happened—it's actually quite rare that I do hear from her. When she first passed on, she appeared to me fully, young, smiling, and dressed as if she were going to Sunday Mass. She only said one sentence: "I found it."

"What did you find?" I asked her.

"Peace," she replied. She smiled, turned, and vanished.

There are so many things the souls have told me over the years that they've learned since they passed into the hereafter that the list would be as long as time itself. I can think of the ones that I have personally found to be important, and perhaps you will also:

Hate is a poison. It destroys everything it touches, including the vessel that contains it.

Guilt and shame are a waste of energy. Sometimes life lessons are designed to humble us. We must accept responsibility, but we must also move on if we are to continue on our journey of understanding.

We are, each of us, on our own journey. As much as we love and care for those around us, we are meant to learn our own lessons and complete the journey we have laid before us.

Love, compassion, and understanding are at the very center of every person's journey on the earth, and they're why we are here. Creating them on the earth is never forgotten by the souls, who regard it as the highest of purposes on the earth, and our most important achievement.

Hurt goes away, eventually. It does not last forever. The pain of loss, the pain of hopelessness, and the pain of disillusionment go away the second we find ourselves in a new world of peace.

Perhaps the most important thing the souls have learned once they cross over to their world in the hereafter is also the most poignant of all: So many of the souls finally realize how much they were loved when they were here. They never realized how much they meant to another, and they didn't know how strongly their presence would be missed once they continued to the world hereafter. So many of the souls are stunned and humbled at how many people regarded them so highly, how many cared, and how many worried after them. They weren't always loved ones or even friends—some were people they did a kindness for, some may have just been passersby in their lives. No matter who we are or what we think, it doesn't seem to register with us just how much we are loved until we see it from such a distant perspective. But the souls realize it is never too late to thank someone for a kindness, or to appreciate someone's concern, or to allow themselves to be loved. It's never too late, because they have all the time in the world to bring peace, hope, and comfort to each of the people who cared so much for them, and they can continue to be a force in their lives, even from the hereafter. The power of love is a chain that can never be broken, and it continues to come and go from the souls to us, and from us to the souls. Of all the things the souls have learned since living in the hereafter, those which deal with love and kindness, to and from others, always stand out in their minds and hearts.

CHAPTER TWO

Relationships

Dear George:

Is there really such a thing as a soul mate?

—Layna

In order to answer this question, we'll have to step back in time a bit to the beginning of the "New Age" movement of the 1980s. Everything that was anything in the world of spirituality seemed to get a face-lift of sorts, and new terms were coined for some of the most basic premises in spirituality. But what these new terms gained in commercial appeal, they lost in specifics—in many cases, the actual meaning and understanding of some of these spiritual principles suffered. Mediumistic ability was suddenly called *channeling*—something I have never understood, because we can't make the souls communicate unless they choose to, but the word *channeling* presumes we have any control in the process. We don't. It was also a time when past life regression was the belle of the ball—everybody wanted to know if they were Cleopatra or Sitting Bull in another lifetime. While past life regression can be a useful tool in understanding some of the issues and phobias we face in this lifetime against the backdrop of past experiences, it somehow morphed into a type of past life treasure hunt. Why we would feel the need to know about a lifetime we already lived and moved on from is beyond me, but it captivated the New Age movement and made a comedy of the science.

While most of what we consider New Age was originally rooted in trying to explain that which may not have an easy answer, the movement itself became a victim of pop culture. It became more about reinventing many ideas outside the comfort zones of the public, and putting them into terms more easily acceptable for those eager for answers but not terribly interested in real education. One of the most over-used and misunderstood terms of the New Age that caught fire—even though it completely changed its actual meaning— was the term *soul mate*.

With the New Age term *soul mate*, we are led to believe that there is one (and perhaps only one) other person for whom we are destined—typically a person for whom we have intense interest, who presumably understands us without our having to speak, and someone for whom we must search relentlessly until we find. While it's all terribly

romantic, it's also terribly *wrong*. I wonder how many relationships were ruined by the phrase, "Well—I like her just
fine, but she's just not my *soul mate*." Soul mate, as it was re-
imagined by the New Age movement, came to be a euphe-
mism for "once in a lifetime love." The actual meaning,
according to the souls, is "pure love," but in a surprisingly
conventional and practical way.

Each of us has had more than one go-round on the earth.
We came to the earth to learn from a specific journey, we
struggled, we triumphed, and we continued on to the hereafter
to live in a world of our own reward. There we stay for eons,
along with the souls with whom we lived on the earth—
parents, grandparents, children, friends, and those whose lives
touched us, and were touched by ours. In some lives of the
souls, the need to return to the earth to learn yet another spiritual lesson arises from wanting to come to even greater understanding, and that soul, after quite a long time of thought and
time in the hereafter, will return to the earth. Some of those in
our generational community may make the trip as well, and
although we were connected by previous circumstances of the
earth, the circumstances of a new lifetime on the earth will
have changed, bringing the same souls to different relationships and connections on the earth. Those who may have been
husband and wife in one lifetime may become brother and sister in this one; those who were parent and child may become
student and teacher; and even those who were adversaries once
upon a time on the earth may become lovers in their new
adventure on the earth. Whatever changes about the roles in

which we find ourselves, one thing remains constant—we were together in another lifetime, we grew spiritually in the world hereafter, and we are back in a related circumstance on the earth. We are *soul mates*—we have a connection that defies definition by only the earth's standards—we are connected in a way that has more history than we may even be able to understand, yet at a very basic and spiritual level, we understand completely that we are connected.

A woman named Rebecca came to see me in session one afternoon, and amid the formalities of introduction, I had to stop her because there was a young man who insisted I begin immediately. I cut Rebecca's statement a little short and told her, "We need to begin, there's a young man here who calls out to you as Mom." As I came to learn many months after the session, my statement to her was one I call "wrong in the mind, but right in the heart." Rebecca was not actually the young man's mother—she was a caring teacher who worked with a troubled youth, and their fondness for each other seemed to come from a place neither of them could fathom in their minds, but they could feel in their hearts. She worked hard with this young man, helping him to overcome obstacles in his personal and educational life. She became very much a parent to him, which seemed to come quite naturally for her, and even more oddly, for him as well—he relied on her just as if she were his mother . . . until an accident ended his journey here. Rebecca related to me that after his passing, she grieved for him just as any mother grieving their own child, and she came to the session hoping for some kind of insight that would help her understand her unique and enduring bond with the young man. His first words, before the session actually even started, were the key to their bond on the earth—he called out to her as *Mom*.

There will be circumstances on the earth were we seem inexplicably drawn to another person like a moth to a flame, because there is something within us that seems to connect on levels we may not always understand. This is the very essence of a soul mate—one who is connected at the soul level, and not always by any measure of the earth. In some lucky instances, our soul mate may very well be our partner or love interest. That in itself doesn't guarantee a lifetime of happiness though—it just connects us, for better or worse, to another soul with whom we have a much deeper understanding and bond.

Because I am a product of the 1950s—my mind goes back to the black-and-white references to life I remember watching on television. My first real understanding of soul mates came while watching Lucille Ball and Desi Arnaz in *I Love Lucy*. Part of their astronomical success as comedians on television was a bond between them that was so palpable, even on a television screen, that made their chemistry seem otherworldly to me and many millions of people. Throughout a stormy marriage, children, divorce, remarriage, and passing, their lives seemed to be so intertwined that it was almost impossible for people *not* to think of them as still married. Although their journey on the earth was not particularly kind to their bond as soul mates, their love did endure, as I believe it does to this day. It's what the souls have frequently referred to in sessions as an "I can't live with you, I can't live without you" conundrum—we seem forever connected, whether we like it or not. The funny thing is, in all the cases where it seems to be a failed relationship on the earth, these relationships always continue in the hereafter—only free of the problems, acrimony, and disappointment that seemed to constantly plague them on the earth.

Not all circumstances of soul mates are stormy, however. Many are just bonds that seem to endure no matter what happens to the souls' individual paths on the earth. One good friend of mine who I met years ago, and subsequently did a session for, had "Father" all around him. Knowing he was single, and not wanting to pry too far into something too personal, I just presented what the souls were telling me. He answered, "No, but I understand." He had a nephew who, estranged from his own father at a young age, drew so close to his uncle that many people naturally assumed they were father and son. That relationship, although they both live their lives and continue as adults, is still as strong and paternal as the day the young man was born. In the session, what I noted from the souls is that they showed me that in another lifetime they actually *were* father and son—so the relationship seems to be a natural continuation from one so long ago, in another world. The dynamics of a love relationship seem the strongest, and endure so much that they follow us into an entirely different lifetime, even if it has to remodel itself to fit within the rigid framework of the world we live in now.

Whatever the circumstance, and no matter the connection, our soul mates are *everywhere*. But that does not always mean we build a relationship around them in this lifetime. Sometimes it's a matter of meeting a stranger on the street, and having the sensation of having known that person somewhere, and somehow. We get the odd feeling of déjà vu, which in French means "already seen"—a very apropos phrase. The connection, indeed, has been *already seen*—in another lifetime, in another circumstance, on another road. But the feeling, the emotion is there. Other times, we have the lucky circumstance of knowing and loving our soul mate in this lifetime as well. Regardless of the circumstance, our connection to the souls we share a community with, both here and hereafter, never changes, and never dies—it continues, as we do—from one life to the next.

Dear George:

Is love predetermined? Are there relationships here that were really "made in Heaven?"

—Laura

This question is one that falls under the "Which came first, the chicken or the egg" header of imponderables, because it all depends on from which angle you look at the lives of the souls. From our own point of view on the earth, it can be difficult to assess how much of our journey has already been planned for us, and how much of the circumstances we live through we are willing to concede are our own doing.

In order to answer the question, I need to explain just how the souls embark on their journey on the earth. Each has told me that before we consider coming to the earth, we create for ourselves a life lesson that will help us grow spiritually and teach us a little more about our own humanity. We create a kind of struggle, an adventure into which we will place ourselves, and then test our ability to love, our capacity to understand, and our willingness to learn from whatever is thrown in our path. The kind of spiritual lessons the souls create are as varied and unusual as snowflakes in winter—each one individual yet common to the human condition on the earth. The issues themselves are very common and universal—some souls will place themselves in a circumstance where they will have to learn humility, some will have to live with the consequences of poor choices, and some may place themselves in circumstances where they will have to learn the importance of how to give and receive love.

Some love relationships here are a very big part of the dynamic of a soul's journey on the earth. It will be their destiny to meet with another soul and form a lasting relationship. Naturally, the same relationship will be part of another soul's journey as well. They meet, they fall in love, and they continue together on their journey. In some of the souls' communication, they have mentioned those they love on the earth, and have spoken in such glowing terms how their loved one was part of their destiny on the earth, and part of their journey of spiritual growth. In a very real way, the relationship was "made in Heaven" because it was essential to the plot of *both* souls' stories. Because the souls come to the earth with their memory of the world hereafter and their spiritual goal wiped from their consciousness, it really does appear to the souls, at least while they are on the earth, that finding true love on the earth was a random and lucky surprise. Many don't realize until after they have returned to the hereafter that it was part of the plan all along. But to the souls, it ultimately makes no difference how or why they came together—they only know that it was among the most beautiful parts of their journey on the earth.

Sometimes, however, the souls will admit that finding love on the earth was a result of their own determination to steer the ship of fate in the direction they wanted it to go— sometimes against all odds and reason—because they believed in their heart that it was where they needed to be. It's completely possible, because each of us has the free will within the confines of our life lesson to bend it to where we believe it *should* go, in order to follow our own path. It's a part of our journey that the souls consider a kind of "free flight" because it requires us to go only by the seat of our pants and rely on our faith and hope that following our heart will be a gamble that will actually pay off. And it does—often in the most poignant and beautiful ways.

Of course, when we think of love, we think mostly of romantic love—something we all, at one time or another in our existence here, will seek out. While the souls don't confine their description of love to only the romantic kind, they do recognize that of all the reasons we will make the decision to commandeer our life lesson and have it move slightly off the rails of our own fate, the search for true love is at the very top of that list. It's the real wild card in our journey here. More has been changed on the earth due to our capacity to love and our seemingly relentless need to create it in our lives here than any other reason. It's the part of our journey where we free-fall, and nearly anything can happen—and often does.

I wonder how often we have altered our life plan to follow our hearts into uncharted and unfamiliar territory—places that were not on the itinerary of our life lesson on the earth. I admit that in this instance, the souls are a bit cagey, because as much as the souls can teach us, we cannot know more about their world than we are allowed while we are still on the earth and struggling to learn on our own. But based on the stories I have heard, from people both here and hereafter, it seems to happen a lot more than we would think. Even the most conservative and cautious of people here will take wild chances when it comes to affairs of the heart. I also think our universe was designed that way. It's our opportunity to take the reins of our fate and take it to places our heart tells us we should be, and it's our opportunity to push ourselves, take chances, and risk failure, if only to just experience something as wonderful and enduring as a lifetime filled with love.

I have heard about nearly every circumstance of life on the earth through the words of the souls—the good, the bad, the truly awful, and the hope-inspiring—but of all the circumstances the souls have lived through, it seems the only thing we carry with us from the earth to the world hereafter is the love we received while we were here. All other emotions seem to fade and disappear—anger, hurt, jealousy, hopelessness— emotions that can overcome us in a far greater way than love. But the love we receive and freely give is the only thing valuable enough for the souls to keep within them when they leave the earth. The souls will often speak in fleeting and completely unemotional terms about troubles they endured on the earth and difficult times they suffered through. When they speak, their recall of often tumultuous events seems so nebulous and remote—like it happened a lifetime ago. But when they get on the subject of love, however, *everything* changes. They speak about their love experiences as if they were part of their here and now. Only love continues to live past the life we know here, and the souls always speak about love—both the good and the bad, both finding it and even losing it, as if it was ultimately the only thing that actually mattered on the earth.

Dear George:

I lost my wife, Suzanne, five years ago to cancer. When it happened I thought my life was over. After being single

for almost four years, I met a lady who I became very
fond of, and now love. I'm at odds over how to tell my
adult children that I want to marry again. I'm especially
worried what my deceased wife will think.

—A.R.

I'm amazed I get this question as often as I do. There seems to be so much needless angst among people, and fear that they may be upsetting somebody in the hereafter simply because they want to do what is perhaps the most natural thing on earth—to fall in love and marry. The souls come to understand that love in the world hereafter is not bound to the conventions of the earth—the rules have changed, and quite frankly, make much more sense.

I have been told by the souls that no matter what the circumstance, our capacity to love has no fixed boundaries or point where it can stop—it keeps expanding to fill the empty places in our heart without any need to define itself. It is possible to love more than one person on the earth, and certainly it is possible that we will love more than one person in the hereafter, but in a much different way. I often help people understand the nature of love in the hereafter by pointing to their children—a parent will have their first child and pour so much love into that child that they couldn't even conceive of loving *anything* as much, let alone another child. Yet another child comes along, and the parent finds that their love just expands to fill the hearts of two children, and because that love is pure, it is possible to love both with equal amounts of love. This is very much the way the souls see the concept of love in the hereafter.

I've often heard in sessions dealing with a bereaved spouse that not only does the soul of their first spouse understand and applaud the effort to continue finding love on the earth, that they also tell us they had a hand in finding somebody to share their spouse's life with. The souls understand, just like parents understand, that love is not confined by such rigid parameters that we find on the earth, but love fills whatever vessel will contain it—freely and without reservation. Having a soul in the hereafter be happy and at peace with your decision to find love again on the earth after the loss of a spouse or significant other shows just how infinite the parameters of love actually are, and how much the souls continue to care for us. Love is never jealous or territorial when it comes to the souls, who always have our best interests and needs at heart.

Dear George:

What have the souls told you about divorce? I'm a Catholic and the Church says it's against God to divorce.

—Gail

This is a question whose answer depends on your belief system and your ability to understand how we are not judged by our choices on the earth, but rather how our choices impact us and the people who are part of our life here.

Religion is not terribly cut-and-dried on the issue of divorce, even though I know that most religions consider it "against God's law" to end a marriage. But like everything else on the earth, there seems to be discrepancies and some wiggle room in nearly every religion that claims to find divorce untenable. In the Roman Catholic Church, for example, Catholics cannot divorce, per se—but they can seek an annulment to a marriage based on some fairly rigid, but still changeable grounds. There are many reasons why some marriages should and need to end—in cases of violence or adultery, or circumstances beyond one spouse's control, as in deception by their partner. People go into unions with the very best of intentions, only to see their spouse change or leave them—physically or emotionally. In the case of personal safety, most religions will allow for a marriage to end because there is the potential for violence. So for all the rigid religious rules regarding marriage and divorce, marriages still do end, and divorces still happen.

The souls have a different take altogether with regard to why some marriages will end in divorce, and how the episode becomes another life lesson in our journey here. They understand that things will happen on the earth, both good and bad, and although we cannot control the life lesson, we can control our own actions. The souls know that clearly not all marriages are happily ever after, and our decision to do what's best for us and the circumstance we find ourselves in is sometimes very personal. The souls know that sometimes the decisions we make, no matter how well intended, are the wrong ones, and finding our way through a bad circumstance and out the other side will be part of our challenge here. Although the souls will try to help us as much as they can by pointing us in the right direction, they also understand that at the end of the day, the decisions we make are ours alone to make, both good and bad.

I had a good friend named Dan a few years back who brought his best buddy to a group session with the man's parents, because he lost his brother to cancer a few years back. The session came on the cusp of the man's impending marriage to his on-again, off-again sweetheart, and the family thought it would be a wonderful idea to hear from the brother and receive his blessings on the upcoming marriage.

What came through in the session surprised me, and shook the family and this gentleman quite a bit. What started off as a very normal session, with the brother communicating about his life in the hereafter, suddenly veered into the soul's need to be candid with his brother. After speaking briefly about himself and his world in the hereafter, the soul told his brother that he was marrying for all the wrong reasons, and that the soul saw disaster. I was startled by how candid this soul was, but I had to repeat what I heard, word for word, for a very shocked man and his parents. At the end of the session they didn't know quite what to say, and neither did I. I know they were angered and put off by the statements, but I heard some weeks later that regardless of what came through in the session, the couple was to be married as planned. Immediately after their honeymoon, they came home, separated, and filed for divorce. I never did learn what the reason was for their separation and divorce, but I could only know from the brother's words that it simply was not to be. In cases like this, which are actually very rare, since the souls do not generally forecast doom, the souls can only suggest to us what the right road is for us to walk—but the actual decision to walk that road is ours alone.

Not all laws make sense—especially when driven by religion. Religion often is the politics of another time and place, meant to instill order in people's lives, but ultimately leaving out the most crucial aspect of life—our humanity. Each of us makes choices in our lifetime based on what we know is best for our journey here. The souls can help us understand a little more about the decisions we are about to make, but they also understand that it is our road to travel the best we know how. They do not judge us, nor does anyone or anything in the hereafter. The choices we make on the earth reflect the life lesson we need to learn in order to advance in our spiritual understanding. The souls know that not every choice we make will be a good one, but they concede that they are also necessary and vitally important to our growth.

Dear George:

Why does love end? I feel like everything I had has been taken from me when my wife left me. How do people go from loving you to nothing?

—Thomas

This is one of those questions that wakes you up in the middle of the night and keeps knocking on the inside of your heart until a suitable answer emerges—if there even is one. I have to be honest, this question threw me a little. I had to think a lot about this question, and I had to wait for some answer from the souls. But the answer came in a simple statement from the souls: "Look at your life. Look at the road."

People wander into our life journey for two basic reasons—to impact our journey here, and for us to impact theirs. While we are a student in our journey, we are a teacher in another's. Sometimes people will bring a valuable and positive experience to our journey, and sometimes the very lesson will be borne of the pain it brings us. As hard as it is to reconcile—we learn equally as much from the positive experiences as we do from the painful ones.

Just as there are happy relationships that stand the test of time, there will be relationships on the earth, also predetermined, that will test our patience, our physical and mental limits, and our very capacity to continue loving in *spite* of the circumstances we find ourselves in. We will never know why somebody who gave their heart to us has the capacity to turn their back on us and stop loving. The most committed relationship can go off course due to fear, insecurity, poor decisions, and lack of understanding. We are all grasping at straws in different times in our lives, and although the road ahead of us seems clear, the way we try to understand our world often isn't. So we make decisions based on what we fear, not what we know. People leave, and for reasons only they can understand—if they themselves even do.

The souls understand from having lived here that sometimes love hurts. They know that something that seemed so right can vaporize in an instant, and our world can go upside down at lightning speed. The souls' advice—to "look at the road"—tells us that we have no actual idea whether what seems so catastrophic now could actually be the best thing that ever happened to us. We don't know, and we fear what we don't know. But the souls know that everything comes full circle for us, and whatever questions elude us here will be found eventually. We need to understand that sometimes the end of love is not the end of our story—it's just a chapter in a book of many chapters yet to come. We need to understand and believe that *everything* we go through has a reason, and has real value to our growth and understanding. No matter how painful, we are better people for having gone through the pain of rejection and the end of a relationship. It is a test of the sheer will of any heart to continue beating after being broken. The souls know that the road ahead of us will be filled with many opportunities to find and share our love—when the circumstance and the time are right. Until then, we have to trust that there is a plan in place—perhaps one we don't quite understand or even accept right away, but we need to try to trust in the fact that what we learn now, no matter how painful, will benefit us in ways we can't even imagine up ahead. One of the things I have learned in my work with the bereaved is that loss—any kind of loss—seems to take away fear. When people lose a loved one to physical death, they no longer fear their own mortality, and sometimes even welcome it. When somebody loses a loved one to the earth, they also lose the fear of having fallen—they already have, and learn that once you understand the pain, you can survive it. It often makes people better at making choices for themselves up ahead, since they are not operating out of a place of fear. It's a hard lesson to learn, but one that brings with it a valued understanding: that once we experience our worst fears, they no longer have the power to control us. My hope is that one day this will have taught you not to fear the end of anything, but to look forward to the beginning of new and wonderful things.

Dear George:

Do the souls believe homosexuality is a sin or is that just man-made? I am in a gay relationship and I would love to know what the souls think of gay marriage.

—Donald

I think before I answer this question, I need to make it clear that the souls don't judge us or our actions; they allow us to judge ourselves, right or wrong. Because of that, the souls don't involve themselves in what is a "sin," because the power to control our own lives and make the decisions we make is part of our learning experience on the earth.

Love is love in the world hereafter, and it's how the souls see our world. How can we say what is right or wrong when it comes to how our heart feels about another human being? The capacity to love is a grace that comes without condition— love sees without color, preference or bias. It's the one thing in each of our lives that we can neither control nor change— love just happens.

When we look at the world as a conglomeration of souls, each on its own journey and each with a purpose to fulfill, it seems silly to expect that love will conform to whatever barriers society throws at it. In a world of souls that see only with their heart, the gender of our intended love seems so much less important than that person's capacity to love. The souls make no mention of whether it is right or wrong, because there *is no right and wrong.* We choose whom we choose based on what our heart tells us, not on what the world tells us. For that reason, the souls only think of us as persons with love to give, looking for a willing recipient of that love, who will, in kind, return it. Past that, the souls have no judgment or advice, other than to be true to who we are, and to love freely those whom we cherish.

Dear George:

I have read your opening web page many times, on which it is stated, "Anything we love, which loves us in return, never dies." This poses a real dilemma for those of us who have lost family that we didn't love, or regarded them as unpleasant burdens. The implication of your quote is that, if we don't love someone—or if no one loves a certain person who has died—then that soul may cease to exist. I hope I'm making myself clear, and would sure appreciate your comments on this conundrum.

Thanks very much,
Charles

This question is only a conundrum because we are human—and we can't see past the arc of this lifetime. With the exception of a rare few, most can't. It's rather like a magazine ad that you first look at that makes no sense at all. Then, somebody comes along and flips open the extender that was folded behind the face page, and there it is—the entire picture. This is how our understanding of life works as well.

Nobody on the earth is unloved. *No one.* And nobody who lived on the earth as a human being lived here without loving another human being. The souls have told me on so many occasions that we are loved beyond our limited understanding, not only by others on the earth, but by the souls themselves. Many of the souls were with us on another adventure on the earth, and chose to stay in the world hereafter while we came back to endure yet another struggle. Even on the earth, those who were the most incorrigible people on earth still found their way into the heart of another human being. We can't even say that we don't love somebody because we hate them, because the opposite of love is not hate, it is *indifference.* The fact that we had emotion for somebody we hated means we had an emotional connection to them whether we liked it or not. Maybe it wasn't our human brain talking, but most likely it was a flash of reason from our soul.

I had a young woman who came to me a few years ago after the loss of her husband in a plane crash. After explaining his circumstance, he rattled off names to his wife that she didn't recognize at all. There were quite a few, and after the first ten or so didn't make any sense, I had to ask him in my mind who the heck these people were. He showed me the plane again, and the faces of the people who died with him that day. He simply said, "At the time of my death, these strangers were my friends, and I loved them all." It's a very powerful statement. Our soul loves what our human form may not.

But, of course, our souls know better, because they are perfect.

Not only are we able to feel love for another human being regardless of what our human failings tell us, the souls themselves love us. Each and every one of us. They love us for our struggle, they love us for our ability to try, they love us for our failures, and they love us for our disappointment. They love us because love is the only antidote for bitterness and disappointment.

So we are loved, all of us. More than we realize. The souls say this so often in sessions I can repeat their words verbatim. We may think we haven't touched another person on the earth, or we may have hurt them with our own failings, but they love us in a way we may never fully understand on the earth. But regardless of what we may think, after looking at an incomplete picture of life here, we know one thing: *Anything we love, which loves us in return, never dies.* Whether we know it yet, or not.

Dear George:

There is a person who has passed on that never knew me and wouldn't recognize me here on earth, but nevertheless,

I did get to know him sort of, from afar, and have felt a strong and deep love for him. I know that might sound silly.

What I would like to know is, is it possible he would know me over there, recognize me somehow, or know that I loved him? What concerns me is that if the hereafter is a reflection of life on earth, is it that only people who got to know each other on earth could get together, see each other, and love each other in the hereafter? Is there any way he might even know I love him now?

Thanks,
Ree

This question is not all that complex, but unfortunately the answer is.

I joke with people that as much as I have been a fan of actress Norma Shearer all my life, she has yet to make an appearance to me or in a session. I often quip to the souls that even though they can't give me any special privilege with regard to the hereafter, I thought I might have enough juice with *somebody* there to give Ms. Shearer the good word about a huge fan. But so far, nothing. So much for thinking communication equals entitlement.

There are two issues at play here, however: The souls know how we feel about them, and may have even been surprised in their life review about how many people may have loved them from afar. The souls have told me that much. They also say they become aware of how they impacted a life here without even knowing it when they themselves were on the earth. I had the opportunity to hear from the soul of John Lennon of the Beatles when a dear friend of his came for a session. In the session, one of the most poignant things Mr. Lennon said was how stunned he was at the outpouring of love and grief after his passing, and how many lives he and his music touched on the earth. He explained that the power of this love was so strong that it lifted into a higher level of spirituality in the hereafter. That is how powerful love can often be. The only thing truly regrettable about it is that we have to wait until we are no longer on the earth to find out such a wonderful secret.

So my guess is that your friend now knows how you feel, since he has returned to the hereafter, and perhaps things will be different when it is your time to finish on the earth and continue on to that world of peace and joy. Love and friendship are not bound and finite like they are on the earth, and when it is your time to pass you may even find that you and your friend may have even shared another lifetime together (which would account for strong feelings now). The answer, for now, is that there is no answer. Just as the souls say endlessly—time will tell.

Dear George:

Does unrequited love ever find resolution when we pass on? I hope so. There is somebody I loved very much, but

*our circumstances kept us from ever being a couple. I
know he loved me, but he had a hard decision to make,
and unfortunately it did not include me.*

—*Karen*

Some of the most poignant moments in sessions come
when a soul pours out his or her heart to a friend or special person who has come to hear from them, to tell them
that they had loved them from afar, and because of circumstances beyond both of their control, they were never able
to experience the kind of love they wanted to while they
were on the earth. We hear so often of "star-crossed lovers,"
but because of things that happen on the earth, and journeys
that may take us away from those we hoped to be with, the
phrase is very real, and sometimes takes a lifetime to understand and accept.

Fortunately for us, the souls, from their vantage point,
understand a lot better why things happen on the earth that
keep us apart from those we truly love and with whom we
felt we were actually meant to be.

People miss the opportunity to entwine their lives for a
variety of reasons. Sometimes it's a sense of duty to another
person and the respect they have for their commitment, and
sometimes it's just a matter of bad timing, where one person
is free while the other is still in the bonds of some entangle-
ment. Mostly, however, it seems that people miss that particular ship because of circumstances in life and on their

journey here that, for reasons we will only understand once we ourselves are in the hereafter, were necessary to their individual soul growth.

Years ago I had a young woman come for a session. When she sat down, immediately a male figure moved forward and put the word *sweetheart*—their symbol of the frilly red heart you'd see on a valentine or the cover of a box of chocolates—over her head. To me this was a sign of great fondness and love. As she acknowledged his presence, the soul quickly moved in and stated emphatically that he was not her husband, but that they were "married in the heart" nonetheless. I had a little trouble understanding how this could *not* be her husband, yet the soul considered them "married." Then the soul communicated about their love being like "two ships that passed in the night" and that he had a bit of a shady past on the earth as a mobster, and considered himself unsuitable to marry someone he loved deeply. The woman wept at his honesty and agreed. She married another gentleman because she knew they could never have a proper life together, but she told me after the session that she had regretted not taking a chance with this man before his passing. "Even a few moments," she explained, "would have been better than holding regret in my heart this many years." But as tragic as this story sounded, it had a bittersweet ending: The soul told her that there would come a day when they would be married, only they would have to wait until they both found each other again in the world hereafter. But he promised that if she could hang on and continue, their lives would come full circle and they would find happiness they somehow missed on the earth, with each other.

It's very difficult for me sometimes to listen to the sessions and not comment as to whether I believe this was right or wrong—being married to one man but pining away for another. But just like the souls, my job is not to judge, but to do the best I can to get the messages across. The woman found great comfort in hearing her beloved say the things she needed to hear, and to me it seems a testament to just how enduring love—even from afar—can be. It's also nice to know that stories like these do have a happy ending—if we are willing to be patient and bear out the journey we have set ourselves upon, and do the best we can until the time comes when we have learned from all our lessons and mistakes, and can continue with a glad heart to whatever, and *whomever*, is waiting with open arms.

Dear George:

My family and I drifted apart (not all of them.) I'm at the point where I'm so fed up, that I don't care if I don't set eyes on them again on this earth! I know I sound really awful. They aren't aware of my feelings, and telling them so would only fall on deaf ears, or they wouldn't give it a second thought. But I want to know that when we reach the other side and go through the life review, will they be made aware of how they've hurt me? I've read in books that when people go through their life review, they see and feel how they hurt others. When we reunite in Heaven, will we ever be close again?

—*Christine*

It's not uncommon for families to fall apart after the loss of a loved one or any other tragic event. People get scared, they don't know what to say, and they abandon their loved ones at the very time they are needed the most. It's human nature, and although it does hurt to be disappointed, that is part of *their* journey. Sometimes people don't always do the right thing. Each of us has the power to decide whether we will do the right thing in any circumstance, or run away from responsibility and care because sometimes it is too hard to do the right thing. Each of us must face these kinds of decisions, and many of us fail in our choices.

In our life review we do get to understand everything we may have done or the times we may have disappointed other people, and how it felt in their heart. So many of the souls tell me that they work very hard to fix what they may have damaged on the earth, so if understanding doesn't come to them in this lifetime, it will certainly come to them in the next. People learn from the mistakes they made on the earth once they enter the hereafter, and each of the souls sets about righting whatever they had done wrong, and whomever they have disappointed with their actions, or lack thereof. But to be honest, once you are in the joy and peace of the world hereafter, it's unlikely it will even matter. Everything comes full circle and the words *I'm sorry* have just as much power in the hereafter as they do here.

Dear George:

Do relationships heal in the hereafter? My mother and I were estranged most of my life, and it wasn't until she was diagnosed with Alzheimer's disease that we were able to repair some of our damaged relationship. But unfortunately, the disease overtook her to the point that she was no longer cognizant of me being there, and we were unable to continue to talk and get to know each other. I have so much pain over the wasted years that we could have been learning to move closer to each other, and I wish we had more time.

—Irene

No relationship is ever beyond repair when people are willing to work on finding peace and love with somebody they may have been estranged from. The souls know that it is never too late to say "I'm sorry," even if they are no longer on the earth, because they hear every word we tell them. They, in turn, find ways to help us find peace in letting go of the past, and looking at repairing old hurts and pain.

There is something very interesting I have learned from the souls with regard to illnesses like Alzheimer's disease: Those suffering from dementia-type brain illnesses have the capacity to be both on the earth and in the hereafter at the same time. Many people who have cared for patients with this type of illness can tell you without reservation that they know when their loved ones were "there" and when they were "elsewhere" by the vacant look in their eyes. It seems that those near the end stages of Alzheimer's are able to visit the hereafter while their body is still alive on the earth. It's an extraordinary revelation from the souls, and it helps us to understand that no matter how badly damaged the brain was, they were able to hear and understand all the things we said to them, but also those things we carried in our heart.

The souls have told me that no matter if they were unable to respond or react during illness, they have heard every word we have told them, and they carried our love and heartfelt messages with them into the hereafter. These souls knew we were there, caring for them, making them comfortable, and telling them all the things we wished we could have said in an earlier time. But again, because it is never too late to say "I'm sorry," the souls know and understand how much they meant to us, and even if they couldn't respond in a way we could understand, were so pleased to hear the words we told them. People always torment themselves needlessly because they were never sure if their loved ones understood how much they were loved, only because they seemed unable to understand or respond.

No matter how incoherent our loved ones may have seemed, every word we told them was registered, heard, and felt in their hearts. Those souls keep the beautiful words we told them in their hearts and hold them for the day they can return them to us, when they see us again in their world.

Dear George:

How do we ask the souls for forgiveness? I was a terrible person to my brother, who was going through a lot of emotional issues just before he passed by his own hand. I find myself struggling to find some peace, and want so much to ask for his forgiveness. How do we find forgiveness of those we love, and forgiveness of ourselves?

—Ron

Not too long ago, there was a woman who came to see me for a session. She had a jovial sense of comedy about her—she really did look like a character actress. Almost before she sat down to ready herself for a session, a male soul bounded into the room and boomed into my brain, "That's my gal." They were two characters—husband and wife, with a real *Pete 'n' Tillie* sense about them. It was a very comical session in spite of the tears, with me telling the wife what her husband was saying, and she, answering him as if she could actually see him in the room.

But the comedy train quickly derailed in no time flat. Her husband, recalling the good times that he was grateful for, as well as the tough times he was sorry for, told his wife through me that she needs to find a reason to continue. And *forgive.* She called out, "I forgive you!" to which he bounded into my head, "Forgive me? Tell her to forgive herself." Hearing that, the woman's face darkened and she said, "What? What is he talking about?" and then she repeated it looking upward, "What are you talking about?"

The session continued, but gone was the good mood and the jovial air. The woman now seemed hollow and deflated in her chair. Her husband tried to reassure her that she would understand why he needed to clearly shake her out of herself and help her the best way he could, but I could tell by the end of the session she had heard more than she wanted to. Her husband, in saying his final thoughts, mentioned again, maybe just for my benefit, "She needs to forgive herself first." Then her husband filled my head and my heart with a depiction of what he was trying to say, if only to help me understand. And I did. That is when I began to really understand how fragile a concept forgiveness actually is.

Forgiveness of others is triumph—somebody knocks you down, you forgive. You get the upper hand, because you decide to forgive instead of holding a grudge. Forgiveness, in a big way, is freedom—it frees you from a bad situation by putting you back in the driver's seat—you forgive, so you win.

Forgiveness of yourself is another matter entirely. It means you have to reckon with the fact that you have done yourself wrong. With no one's help. So there is no upper hand. It's easy to say we forgive our loved ones for the petty grievances we had with them while they were on the earth, even if those grievances were not so petty. But there is an ugly side to forgiveness we need to face, especially after a loss—how do we forgive ourselves for what we feel?

In sessions, I'm often privy to information nobody would ever even think about discussing under normal circumstances. Like the couple I mentioned earlier—things went so well, until that ugly concept was tossed into the fray. The woman's husband showed me why his words stung his wife so much—and it was startling to me. She hated him. She loved him, but she hated him, too. She hated having to live alone. She hated not having a partner she could share her advancing age with. She hated him for leaving first. She hated her life right now, and she hated God for ruining the only good thing in her life. She hated. And worse than that—she hated herself for feeling that way.

There will come a time in each of our lives when ugly, dark thoughts will emanate from us. We will taste the bitter acid of hatred. We will feel anger. We will go from understanding people's compassion to hating their silly cheer-ups and self-serving platitudes. We'll hate our best friends for not feeling the same pain we feel. We'll even hate those we truly love, because we can't stand the thought of another loss ripping away what is left of us.

To forgive ourselves is having to turn that warped mirror around, to see our own sad reflection in it. But each of us needs to look within and try to understand the struggle with ourselves the same way another would understand it, if it were caused by somebody else. We need to look at ourselves as somebody who failed us—who caused us anxiety, fear, panic, and loathing, and then turn right around and at least try to understand ourselves enough to forgive what we put ourselves through.

Our grief can be a cruel partner for as long as we will allow it. But just like with the person who knocked us down, who gave up, who failed us, who hurt us, we can find it within ourselves to say, "I forgive. I forgive myself." I forgive the fact that I hate being bereaved. I forgive myself for feeling lonely as a result of my loss. I forgive myself for not being able to connect with friends and relatives the same way I could before my loss. I forgive myself for being jealous of somebody else's happiness. I forgive myself for blaming my hate on somebody else. And most important—I forgive myself, because had it been done to me by anybody else, I would have easily forgiven them. I deserve forgiveness, and I give it to myself.

We learn so much about ourselves on the road to recovery after any tragic circumstance on the earth. Not all of it is good, but all of it is important. I don't think there is a more important lesson that the souls can teach us than to learn how to forgive ourselves for whatever we have done to ourselves and those around us because we are in pain. We can't hope to move on to a perfect world if we can't see the importance of setting ourselves free from guilt, from anger and from pain. To forgive ourselves is to fix the soul, and lighten the load here just enough to be able to continue our journey of hope.

Dear George:

Do the souls really know how much we love and miss them?

—Robin

In more than forty years of working with the souls, the one thing I know for certain is that no matter what becomes of us on the earth, love is the most powerful and enduring of the emotions. Love has the power to extinguish hate, jealousy, and fear, and lives on even when the physical body dies. Love is the only thing the souls bring with them to the hereafter, so that they can shower those they love on the earth with all the love they have collected from each of us during their time on the earth. Love is more powerful than death.

The souls know how much they mean to us, and that they were loved beyond their limited understanding when they were on the earth. Now, in a world of total clarity, they can see straight into our hearts and understand, perhaps for the first time, the depth of love we feel for those we cherish. The souls don't feel the same pain of separation as we do, because they are able to be with us during those dark moments when we think we are all alone, and they have the ability to comfort our hearts, in order to help us find our hope and a reason to continue on in our journey here. But the souls also understand that part of our spiritual lesson on the earth is to endure the pain of a loved one's passing, and they cannot take that pain away from us, for fear of taking away a large part of the reason why we are still here—to learn to love again and continue to find hope and peace while we suffer the loss of a loved one. The souls want so much for us to complete the lessons that are to be among our greatest struggles here, so that we may enter the hereafter when our work on the earth is done, and join them in a world of joy. To the souls, it is only in the blink of an eye that they will see us again, but to us, it is day after day of working to earn the same love, joy, and peace that the souls now find in their new world. In the meantime, the souls have never left our side; they continue to walk with us, share our joy and pain, and continue helping us to help ourselves until we see them again. This is how powerful their love for us is: they spend the rest of our lives caring for us in ways we may never completely realize until we see them again and understand from their unique perspective. But no matter what time or distance separates us from those we love, we hold a piece of them in our hearts, and we hold an invisible thread that connects us to their love and hope. This is something the souls have promised each and every one of their loved ones on the earth—that they will never abandon us, because their love for us is as steadfast and enduring as the Infinite Light itself. One fine day we will be able to see our loved ones again and return the love they gave us so freely as they helped us navigate the rest of our existence here. The souls' love for us is like a beacon that will lead us right back to them when our work on the earth is done.

CHAPTER THREE

Falling Down

Dear George:

I have followed your career with great interest for a long time. I've heard you use the term "falling down" a lot to describe our life here. What is it about that term that seems to reflect what the souls have told you about life here?

—Alfred

In a lot of the communication I've had with the souls, much of the information comes—just like education comes to each of us—by example, by revelation, and sometimes by witnessing important lessons as they happen. "Falling down" is a way the souls help us understand that sometimes we will experience failure in our lives, or an inability to continue walking through the journey of our lives. Falling in our faith, hope or beliefs will be a part of each of our lives. And although it happens at some point to each of us, it seems that nobody but the souls want to address it. No matter who we are, what we do, or how secure we are in our lives, we will all fall down at one point or another.

One minute, we are moving blithely through our lives, we are dealing, we are understanding, and the next—without any warning, we are down, the wind has been knocked from us, and the entire world is spinning.

What happened? The problem is that danger lurks all around us—the danger that threatens our well-being and our hard-fought survival after a tragedy, during a setback, or just living day to day. Because we don't immediately see it, it doesn't mean it isn't there. The ground under our feet is not always solid, the balance in our world is not always stable, and the road in our lives is not always smooth. So we go fine for a while—we live, we work, we grow—until we fall. What we do next is really a testament to the people we are, and a defining moment in our own learning experience on the earth. Falling down, and then picking ourselves up and continuing, perhaps more humbly, is among the greatest things we will learn while we are on the earth.

My interest and fascination with the term *falling down* as it relates to facing times when we will fall short of our own goals and lessons, came in the form of a rather graphic lesson I experienced one cold day in December, nearly ten years ago. I still remember with an awful feeling in my stomach that cold winter night I came back home with my coauthor, Andrew, after a nice and well-earned after-work dinner. I parked the car in front of my garage, and Andrew leaped out of the car and onto what we found was a driveway covered in black ice. He went down hard, and the sound his head made when it hit the pavement was sickening.

I rushed over to his side of the car to find him lying on the ground with wide eyes, and I panicked. I told him, "Don't get up!" but he started scrambling to his feet the best he could after such a hard fall. I didn't want him to move; I wanted to call my doctor friend to just check him for anything serious before he attempted to get up. But Andrew wouldn't have it. He got back on his feet, a little at a time—first to his knees, then slightly bent, and then upright and clinging to the side of the car as we sort of stumbled together to safer ground.

Later on, as a precaution, the doctor did examine him to make sure there was nothing worse than a bump on his head, and thank goodness he was fine. But I thought about the way people react to the simple, scary act of falling down—and how they deal with it—seems to define the very essence of who they are. When our circumstances throw us down, do we panic? Do we remain immobile? Or can we find a reason to get back up for another try?

We seem to be strolling along fine until something pulls the rug out from under us, and we find ourselves falling— falling from the small spot of understanding we have built. We fall when we encounter struggles in our lives, or from the weight of too many hard-to-deal-with circumstances in too short a time. We struggle, we throw our arms out to steady ourselves, but we fall. What we do next defines us as human beings. Do we struggle to get up? Do we just stay there? Do we ask for help, or do we give up and stay down?

No matter how steady you are in dealing with the myriad of issues we all face as part of our lessons on the earth, there will be times when you will fall. The struggle may be just bearable, but there may be an incident that takes the whole show down with you. We deal with problems in our lives every day, but there will be times when the issues snowball and overtake an already burdened soul. Maybe right now, while you are still standing, is a good time to make a contingency plan for the next time you fall hard. Maybe now would be a good time to think about what it will take to pull yourself up and off the ground when it happens.

Because of my work with the bereaved, I have personally seen people who have fallen in their grief, and refuse to get up. It's too hard, so they stay down. And they lose the rest of their lives. But it's not just the bereaved who fall. It's anyone who has tried hard but has still experienced failure in life or work. I've seen others, who, in their effort to pretend the fall didn't happen, get up too quickly, and risk falling down again even harder. So maybe the thought of a contingency plan for how exactly to get back up warrants some consideration. For this, we can look directly to the souls and their words.

Firstly, if you think too much about falling, you *will* fall. Conversely, if you never even consider the possibility of falling, life will do it to you anyway. So now that we find ourselves on the ground, wide-eyed and in shock after a sudden failure, what's next? The souls say that the struggle to find our way back onto our feet is part of our life's lesson here. Sometimes, in lucky circumstances, we will have help. But sometimes, like my friend Andrew, it's best to just slowly try to test each step you take as you struggle to get back on your feet. If you stay down, nothing will get better. At least if you struggle back, you have a fighting chance of succeeding. We need to produce the hope and the determination to create enough energy to undo the damage of our fall, and look for ways to put the pain, the humiliation, and the scare of falling behind us. The funny thing is that after it is over, it is forgotten, and we continue on as if we had never fallen before. Sure, we may have a bump or two, but we are back, and walking again. And our hope gives us one good lesson: We lived through the fall and we got back up and walked.

Dear George:

I know this seems like a strange place to pour out my heart because you work with people who lost loved ones, but I was wondering if the souls ever give you advice about what to do when your world has come crashing down around you. I'm a fifty-five-year-old male who, like many people caught in the financial bubble of recent times, saw his finances nearly completely disappear in the stock market. I am semi-retired and just a few months ago I thought I had it all. Now I feel like I have been ruined, and frankly, I'm scared to death. Do the souls have any advice for people like me? People who worked hard to make something of themselves and achieve a certain level of success only to have it all taken away?

—*Mike*

I've heard from the souls and what they have to say about nearly every aspect of life on the earth over the past forty-plus years, and I have to tell you that sometimes the souls will dispense with the pretty words and flowery phrases to shake us up a little and bring us back to a place where we can begin thinking again—not just about our problems, but about our ability to be flexible, our ability to see things as opportunities and not just setbacks, and to dropkick us back into the reality we need to face in order to continue on our journey here.

Loss is loss—whether it's a loved one, possessions, money or social standing. We grieve over what we have lost, and part of the healing comes from grieving and recognizing that we have been laid low by a particular circumstance. But although the circumstances that bring us loss may vary greatly, the advice from the souls doesn't vary all that much—except to perhaps realign our thinking so that we can begin seeing possibilities where we think none exist. Because of that, you may find some surprise in the words the souls have to say about financial loss. You may not like to hear all of it, but I wouldn't be doing my job if I tried to soft-sell or sugarcoat anything the souls have to tell us. They say what they say for a reason, and sometimes just in the way they say things, we can understand why and how they come to what they want to tell us. It's generated out of a place of concern by the souls, but also because they lived on the earth, they know fully well the reality of living here and the danger of becoming too self-absorbed in our own despair to dig ourselves out. So the souls' advice will be a little different in dealing with a loss to the earth than it would be to someone experiencing a loss to the hereafter.

The souls generally ask people to really think about what they are saying when they say they have *"lost it all"* in regard to financial setbacks. The souls are going to fight you on this, and tell you as a matter of fact that you have *not lost one thing* that is important in your life, or in your journey, for that matter. What you've lost is your pride. And perhaps a little of the arrogance we invariably and sometimes unconsciously gain as a result of having a little too much pride, or looking at our accomplishments in life as a matter of dollars and cents.

The souls know from having lived here that sometimes life will gently move us from the direction we are going in, because it is not the journey we signed on to take. If that doesn't work, then life will buffet us about the head, completely humiliate us, and leave us with no other choice but to walk in the direction of the road we have just been thrown on to. Money is one of those things that is a game changer in many lives and many journeys on the earth. When we have it, it comes with its own special circumstances, issues, problems, joys, and sorrows. But conversely, when we *don't* have it, it comes with its own special circumstances, issues and problems, but also *opportunities*. Somewhere, somehow, the universe is telling you that you are not on the path you need to be, and that you need a *bonfire of the vanities* to shake you out of complacency, and back into the real work of what was supposed to be your journey. It's never easy, but it is necessary if we are going to complete the lesson we were supposed to have learned while we were here. The lesson is so important to our spiritual growth that sometimes the souls are merciless in removing the things that became soft, lovely obstacles to our true path in order to bring us back to where we should have been. And we have choices—we can be pushed back to our journey, kicking and screaming all the way, or we can actually look at our new circumstances as a way of reinventing ourselves and finding a new and better way to seek out the lessons and experiences we were supposed to be learning before the lovely car we were driving drove straight into the mud.

So what will it be? What can the souls expect of you? As I mentioned before, the souls will not sugarcoat advice about vanity, arrogance or pride. And their advice is always quite clear when it comes to financial loss: get back up; stop crying over what you think you have lost, because you have not lost one thing important to your life here; and do it all again. But this time, you will be doing it with the understanding that pride doesn't come from what you've earned, it comes from what you've done. You have an opportunity to rebuild nearly your entire life from the perspective of what is supposed to be your learning experience here, and the souls' advice is always to take the lead they have given you, and do it again. The real measure of any human being's worth is not if they have fallen, but if they can get back up, and understand just why and how they fell. I and the souls have real faith in you—you'll do well. Make us all proud—find a reason to begin again, and a way to use everything you have experienced and learned from up to this point to be the model of your next success.

Dear George:

I have found myself praying to the spirits a lot lately, and I thought who better to ask my question to than a man who regularly hears from them?

I just find myself at a crossroads in my life, and it's beginning to wear on me to the point that I have trouble getting through my day. Here is the simple truth: I feel unfulfilled as a wife and mother. It's a terrible thing to say, I know, but, George, I had such dreams and plans when I was a young girl. Please don't get me wrong, I love my children and my husband dearly, but I thought there would be more. More of me in my life. I know I probably need psychological help, but I have read some of the things you write to others and you have always been so inspired by the spirits, I thought perhaps they may have some advice for me.

—Carole

Before I answer this question, I have a question of my own: Why are people so ashamed of being completely honest with themselves? There is absolutely nothing wrong with finding the courage to tell yourself and the people around you that you don't really feel like you have realized your full potential on the earth, and that your journey seems slightly off its actual path. I think part of the problem comes from either locking ourselves, or having others lock us into a single function on the earth—I am Mom, or I am Wife, or I am Partner. We are so much more than just the sum of our functions that its almost inevitable that at some point we will realize that the other pieces of our lives have not been dusted off in quite a long time. Wanting to realize those parts of us that want more is not something we should hide or fear. It doesn't make us less that we don't want to be tied to one function in our lives, but rather, it makes us *more* that we want to explore and live through every part of what makes us unique and human.

The souls tell me frequently through sessions that any part of our lives unrealized is a part of our lesson unlearned. And because we are not learning all we need to know with regard to our journey here, there will be the feeling of being unfulfilled by the parts we have managed to keep moving. It doesn't make those other parts any less valued and valuable, but it would be rather like a book with chapters left unwritten. The souls know that the key to our success in our lives and in our life lessons lies in understanding who we are, who we have been, and what the potential is to be who we know we want to be. I believe that just being able to recognize that there are unopened chapters of our lives, or chapters cast aside by more pressing parts of our lives, is the beginning of a journey of self-discovery.

One of the most difficult things I hear from the souls when they communicate is their regret at not having done more for themselves or to fulfill their spiritual path on the earth. Yes, they do go to the hereafter and find the peace that had eluded them, but they do concede that it would have been nice to have a life fully realized on the earth *before* their transition. Souls just like you who gave up on their dreams in favor of responsibilities now look at those times and shake their heads, wondering why they just didn't put aside the fear and guilt, and just grab their happiness here with both hands. It's a rather remarkable thing to hear from the souls, because, in retrospect, they saw how *easy* it was, once the fear, uncertainty, and guilt were removed. The souls often wonder what the fuss was all about. Hindsight being twenty-twenty, I suppose it is easy from their vantage point to figure it all out, but their wisdom and their understanding about their life on the earth should teach us a thing or two about taking chances and rolling the dice, even if we think circumstance has made our decision for us.

It *hasn't*. Our fear often makes the decision to not continue to pursue things we love, things we want to accomplish, and people we want to be. It's a sad commentary on the lack of faith we have in ourselves.

While we are on the earth, we need to reach our arms out to all four corners of our experiences and lessons on the earth—the good, the bad, the wonderful, the tragic—because it makes us the fully rounded souls we will become once our work here is done. The souls have said many times to me that although we love our spouse, our children, our family and friends, each of us is on our own individual and unique journey, and no one's journey, no matter what the circumstance or relationship, is more important than our own. That's a hard statement for many family people to hear, but it is absolutely the truth. Our children cannot finish our spiritual education for us, and our spouses, friends or extended family cannot learn our spiritual lessons for us. Our journey is ours alone to accomplish, and it cannot be done for us. It certainly cannot be done by involving ourselves so much in another's journey that we lose our way in our own. Each of us can be son, daughter, husband, wife, child, parent, friend, and relative—and still accomplish the goals we set out to achieve in order to give ourselves the most comprehensive educational experience we can have on the earth. It's up to us—it's up to *you*. Live the life you chose for yourself, and live in every room of the house you built for yourself on the earth.

Dear George:

I'm sure you won't remember me but I came to see you about three years ago when my wife, Sylvia ("Sylly" if you remember the session) passed away. She had so much to tell me that was helpful, and I was hoping perhaps she may have some words of wisdom for me now. I just recently lost my job, a job I did for thirty-eight years. Well I didn't quite lose it, I was in effect "put out to pasture" for lack of a better term. That job was really all I had, and now I feel lost and without direction. No job, no Sylly, it's been hard, George. I don't feel "old" and I want to work. Nobody will give a man in his sixties a job that has any dignity, and believe me I have tried hard. Maybe Sylly has some words of encouragement that can help me from feeling so down in the dumps lately. I sure hope so.

—Gary

I certainly do remember this session because I honestly thought his wife was making fun of me by calling me *silly*, when she was just trying to get her nickname across. I thought to myself at the time, "Geez, the souls are getting a little cranky with me," but she made it clear (thankfully) that *she* was "Sylly" and not me. Well, at least, not at that moment.

I recall his wife telling me that Gary was a little on the sensitive side, and that sometimes it led to trouble for him. She said that he "had his feelings a little too close to the surface." Maybe if we can understand what she meant we could understand why Gary found himself at this crossroads in his journey.

One thing the souls seem to understand completely from their perspective in the hereafter is how fragile the human ego can be. Now that they have let go of that particular kind of turmoil—the struggle to maintain a strong sense of ourselves—they can see with much more clarity than we can. While we tend to get badly affected by the "box" or category our society and the people around us may put us in, the souls know that who we are as human beings is so much more important. We are so much like eggs—we may have a tough exterior, but one blunt strike and everything gooey from within us bleeds out. We find ourselves as irreparable as that shell that contained all our insecurities and fears. And this feeling comes as we feel everything else slipping from us, especially when we reach a certain age. Why age and ego are so hopelessly entangled is something *only* the souls can help us understand.

I vividly remember about twenty years ago when I went to the movies to see a digitalized and improved version of

Gone With the Wind with two friends at one of those art house cinemas New York City is famous for. My hair started graying in my late twenties, so by my thirty-ninth birthday, I was fully gray. It never bothered me because I thought it was stylish and cool, particularly since I stayed active and was in good shape. My wonderful opinion of myself quickly disintegrated when the box office employee handed my friends two full-price tickets, and handed me a discounted senior citizen ticket. At first I thought she had simply made a mistake and I pushed the ticket back to her through the small opening in the window. But she pushed it back at me with two dollar bills and said, "Seniors are half price, Pop." I was stunned, and I'm sure at that moment my face was as ashen as my hair. I sheepishly picked up my ticket and the two dollars and moved away from the counter. What actually made it worse for me is that my poor friends did not even dare to laugh—I think they were embarrassed for me. I felt humiliated, and for the first time in my life, I felt as if the whole world viewed me as *old*.

That experience was a long time ago, and in terms of my spiritual education courtesy of the souls, seems almost a lifetime away from where I am now. But it led to a very valuable lesson. Among the really important things the souls have taught me personally, one of the most important is that the measure of any human being is what they have learned about *themselves*, not what they fear. We worry way too much about what things *look like* instead of what things actually are. It's our perception that is lacking, not our reality.

When I read Gary's letter, I could tell he was feeling alone and vulnerable, and it is understandable, to a point. But it is only his perception. I remembered him to be in very good shape and good health—two things that he seemed to be overlooking. Yes, he was of a certain age, and yes, the world looks at the aged differently. But that is the world's issue; it should not be his. The souls know that no matter what our physical age, the best moments in our learning experience are always ahead of us, if we could only trust them and understand. There will always be another experience to be had and another opportunity to move us closer to complete understanding of why we go through the things we do here. The souls have dispensed with the notion of *ego* because they are surrounded by love, understanding, encouragement, and approval. Us, not so much. We have to create it within ourselves, and try to listen carefully, especially when loved ones like Sylly whisper to us that we are better now than we ever have been, because life has taught us to be resilient. We are not eggs. Gary did not crumble into nothingness when Sylly passed on, and he should not crumble now that he has been presented with an opportunity to find another direction both in work and in life.

We all need to be careful of the ego, and be careful about using words like "dignity" and "respect." There is nothing dignified about being the president of a major corporation if you are a sham, but there is plenty of respect to be had for an older person who works at a fast-food restaurant and shares life experiences and work ethics with teenaged coworkers who may be long on ego, but rather short on much else. One of the most valuable lessons I learned from my own parents is that it is not the job that makes the man, but rather, the man who does his job well, no matter how that job is perceived by the rest of the world. Bringing excellence to whatever you do in work and in life is its own measure of success—especially to the souls and our own spiritual growth here. Nobody asked the souls in the hereafter what kind of job they did on the earth—but rather, how they poured their heart and soul into whatever they did. That is the real measure of our success on the earth, and something far more valuable to our journey than our fancy job or title. Our work, and how we choose to do it, makes us important, not just in our own eyes, but in the eyes and hearts of others.

So here we find ourselves on our journey—advancing in years, graying, and perhaps having our egos bruised and our vanity dented. If we want approval, we are certainly looking in the wrong place. We need to define ourselves by what we want to accomplish, not how the uninformed around us try to guess at what or who we are. The souls will never stop trying to help us understand, but it is up to us to take down our shaky wall of pride long enough to allow them to fill our hearts with hope. No matter what we do or who we are, the only approval we need to seek is that of the souls of the people we love, who will continue to fill us with whatever assurances we need to continue, if we allow them to speak, and if we allow ourselves to listen.

Dear George:

I desperately want to hear from the souls because I feel like a bad person, and I wish somebody would understand. My husband has heart disease and many physical ailments that have basically rendered him an invalid. For more than two years, our wonderful life has disappeared, and life now is filled with hospitals, doctor appointments, and having to care for him twenty-four hours a day, seven days a week. He hasn't worked in quite some time, and even with my part-time job we are in danger of losing our home and everything we worked so hard for. I just feel like a terrible person because I hate this—I hate what has happened, and I hate the fact that this was supposed to be some of the best years of our lives. And now we're broke, he's sick, I'm tired, and life has been terrible. Did I somehow bring this upon myself? Maybe I am being punished? If there is any information the souls could tell you, I would appreciate it, even if it's knowing that I only have myself to blame for my and my husband's misfortune.

—Kelly

At the risk of seeming insincere, I have to say that after reading this letter, my thoughts first wandered to a skit by the famed British comedian Rowan Atkinson. In the skit, he is dressed as a pastor who is addressing his flock with a parable:

> *They brought him on a stretcher—a man who was sick of the palsy.*
> *And they cried unto Him, "Lord, this man is sick of the palsy." And*
> *the Lord said, "If I had to spend my whole life on a stretcher, I, too,*
> *would be SICK of the palsy."*

Sometimes humor is the only way we can decompress such serious issues, and hopefully find some humanity in being able to find a funny moment in an otherwise painful circumstance. I thought of the comedy skit because there is a truth in the humor—of *course* we get sick and tired of the very hard work of caring for somebody who is seriously ill and permanently debilitated. Admitting such is honest and candid, and Kelly's e-mail shows a real willingness to listen to and understand what the souls are trying to tell us about the difficult circumstances each of us will face in our lifetime on the earth.

Nothing drains our hope and faith faster than the emotional pain and physical work of caring for someone who is ill. Not only can it be backbreaking work, but the toll it takes on our emotional well-being has the capacity to render us completely hopeless. There, without hope, physically tired and worried, our minds begin to conjure all kinds of thoughts about how we may have "earned" this terrible situation we find ourselves in. We look for times we may have been short with someone, or unkind—anything we can to feed the frenzy in our minds that somehow we *deserve* what has been put upon us. Nothing else on earth has the capacity to ruin our hope like the thoughts in our own heads, and it seems tragic that on top of everything else—with life seeming to beat us down—we help by finishing the beating ourselves.

I know that the souls are their most compassionate when they see us struggle, not only with the circumstance we find ourselves in, but when we begin to beat ourselves up for our own honesty. We are not saints, and not even the saints were saints when they were on the earth—they had good days and bad, they had irritations and annoyances, they had struggles and pain. In short, they were *human* and they grappled with their occasional crises of faith and hope just like we do now. Many people forget that Jesus was so enraged at seeing money change hands in the temple that he overturned tables. Francesca "Mother" Cabrini was so enraged at the fishmongers in the Lower East Side of New York charging poor immigrants a higher price on their fish that she threatened to burn down the fish market in protest. So when you have a bit of an episode where you fall down in your hope, please remember that you are in *very* good company.

One of the biggest issues I have heard from people who have tended to sick and terminally ill loved ones is that the job was mostly thankless, and that there was never any opportunity to share the fact that it is very hard work. You know firsthand that there is often little sleep to be had, backbreaking work and problems that would test the patience of the Infinite Light itself. But we do it—we do it because we know it needs to be done, and more important, we do it because these are people we love and want to care for. I wish more people were honest about the struggle to care for a loved one and the fact that while heroic, it seems not terribly important to anyone other than the recipient of care. I also wish caregivers would band together, if only to commiserate *and* congratulate each other on their strength, endurance and patience. But aside from just offering some vague platitudes of encouragement, I want to tell caregivers what the souls say about their particular journey on the earth, and why they were chosen for one of the most difficult life lessons on the earth.

Many of the souls who have communicated to me came from a life of struggle that they can only now begin to comprehend and understand the value of. They seem to draw especially near to those who find themselves in similar struggle, and at the very least, try to provide some kind of spiritual support and encouragement to people who are trying the best they can to help another through illness. One thing the souls have learned from their own experiences is that we are thanked in ways we can't even begin to imagine when we ourselves graduate to the world hereafter. The struggle we chose for ourselves as a life lesson before we even came to the earth is to understand that the very nature of love is giving ourselves to others, and in caring for a loved one who is ill, it isn't just a sense of duty that makes us feel we have to do it—it's an expression of the highest form of love we can give to another. It may not ever be acknowledged in a way that would make the job any easier, but each second that we set aside our own needs for another is recorded in the account of our life on the earth. If you are a caregiver, know that you have been heard, you have been seen, and you have been forgiven for the temporary wavering of hope that comes with exhaustion and worry. This is completely the reverse of the "punishment" you may think you are receiving. You were asked to do a job as a part of your journey on the earth, and you have done it with a glad heart and a true willingness. When you feel yourself sagging under the weight of the burden you have been asked to carry, remember the love. Find a way to make yourself understand that as hard as it is, you would do it all again if asked, because the love we have for another brings us the strength to see us through the problems, the struggles, and the pain. The souls understand you more than you can imagine, and have helped perhaps a little more than you realize. Try to remember that none of your hard work is thankless—you will be thanked, in ways that may surprise you, both on the earth and once your journey is done and you move on to the hereafter. Nothing done in love for another is ever forgotten by the souls or the Infinite Light—your investment of time, love, and compassion will pay off for you in ways the souls have now learned. You have been heard, and you are not going through your struggle alone. When you feel overwhelmed, just remember the love, and ask the souls for that little bit of strength to push past your fear and anguish, until the world begins to make sense again. We all get "sick of the palsy," but we never forget the reason why we signed on for such a difficult task—love.

Dear George:

I read the questions people post to you on Facebook and your answers, which seem so inspired and honest. I knew I needed to ask you for help, but I wouldn't dare post my question on a public website because of the sensitive nature of it. Do the souls ever talk about what happens to people to make them change so much during their life? I love my wife so much, but she's become indifferent to me and I fear she no longer loves me. I know she cares about me, but things are very strained—she isn't intimate anymore, if you know what I mean, she cries a lot, and we don't talk like we used to. I know this isn't about bereavement and it isn't your area of expertise, but she is my life and I don't want to lose her. Maybe God has some kind words for me, too.

—Denver

I often think that asking a bachelor like me for advice about relationships and affairs of the heart is about as crazy as asking the local priest for help with a sexual issue. But then the souls remind me of the many sessions where they spoke with such clarity about love and relationships that I feel a little bit better about dispensing *their* advice, since my own, as a bachelor, would be rather worthless. But each of us has the capacity to love, and although we may come together and sometimes fall away from each other in the course of a lifetime here, there are so many things we can take to heart from the wise words of the souls, no matter what kind of relationship we have.

One thing I have learned from listening to the souls is that anything that can come together can also come apart. It's inevitable that over the course of a lifetime, as we grow, change, and learn in our experiences, relationships with others may get tested, mainly because we all change and grow at different rates. Relationships with friends, family, and those we choose as a love interest are all living things—they expand and contract, they change shape and form, and they sometimes wind up in entirely different places than where they started. Sometimes, as our experiences on the earth reshape our thinking, we may begin to differ in ideology and interest from what we felt perhaps months and years ago. We *change*, and sometimes it may be for the better, or sometimes it may be for the worst. Life does funny things to people on their road here—some experiences will leave people with a better understanding of their life and purpose here, and other experiences may leave people brittle and inflexible. This is where the souls can be their most helpful, because they see the panorama of a lifetime on the earth as an arc that has a beginning and end, and a clear line that connects them both. They have experienced the very things we some-times must wander aimlessly in the dark about, and they understand why each of us goes through periods of flux. Our journey here is never static—it's constantly moving and changing as we move and change, so everything in our lives that we want to keep may have to find a measure of real flex-ibility in order not to fall apart. This seems especially true with marriages and love relationships.

One of the biggest issues the souls have about people on the earth is that we talk, but we don't *say* anything. We also hear, but somehow we don't actually listen. We have fallen down in perhaps the most important aspect of our life on the earth—communication. So often we are told by a spouse or love interest what they feel, only to turn it back on them or ourselves and make it a singular issue rather than a joint problem. We're too busy listening to the buzzwords that push our buttons based on our own insecurity that we don't think of our problems as something outside of ourselves that sometimes need only attention and thought.

The souls have often found so many instances in their own lives on the earth where they could have said the things they knew would help, but somehow fear got in the way. I always find it sadly ironic that near the end of a physical life on the earth, when there is almost no time left, people become the most honest they ever were, and tell loved ones how much they meant to them, what a joy it was to be with them, and how life would never have been the same without them. True, they are poignant and necessary words, but why do we wait for the last possible minute to tell people exactly what they meant to us and the fabric of our lives? This is where many of the problems in relationships seem to lie— we simply do not speak the right words until we find the wrong time.

It seems in sessions that the biggest regret most people have is that they feel they never had the opportunity to say what they truly meant to loved ones. They dance around issues, they try to show it in different ways, but they don't actually *say the words*. I remember reading a medical study years ago that people wearing a heart monitor were told the words *I love you*, and they were able to see the visible affect it had on their heartbeat. I always found that to be amazing— three simple words that could literally affect the heart in a palpable way. We take for granted things that we think are implied. We are married, so of course we love each other. We share a bank account, so of course we are committed to each other. We share a life together, so of course we were meant to be. But when are the words actually said? Sadly, they are said when a loved one passes, and you can only hear their response in your heart. The souls know this firsthand—they see the heartbreak of those still on the earth with so many things left unsaid, with so many moments uncherished, and with so many opportunities to make somebody feel good about themselves left undone. In my work, I see the anguish every day. Of course the souls can hear us, and they know exactly what is in our hearts with regard to how much we love them, but being able to not only say but demonstrate our affection, commitment, and love is so precious that we need to think about it all the time. And we need to express it as if this were our last minute to say what we know needs desperately to be said.

Another thing I have learned from the souls is just how carefully they listen to everything we tell them. The souls can recount the times we thought of them, worried about our problems, and all the times we have asked for their assistance. They have heard every word. How many of us can say we listen—really *listen*—to the things the significant people in our lives tell us? Perhaps now is the time in your relationship, as you feel each other growing away from your foundation, to bring it back together by *talking* and *listening* to each other? Not just the words, but the intent. People become unhappy most of the time because they feel they are not understood. Everybody in their journey here wants to understand and be understood—it's the very core of our existence here. As I said before, I am no relationship expert, but I am an expert in communication. When I listen to the souls, I have to really *listen* to them because I have a responsibility to their loved ones here to report everything I can possibly tell them from their loved ones in the hereafter. Were that we all could be that careful and responsible every day with the people who matter to us—that we speak clearly and with intent, and that we listen even more carefully, not just to the words, but to the meaning behind them. If you are struggling in a relationship, you should practice playing the part of a medium. I have no psychic ability, so I cannot guess or intuit what the souls want to tell me. Unless I listen to them, I have no way to know what they want to tell me. Nobody should have to guess how their loved ones feel about them, and nobody should ever feel that love and commitment is "implied." We are not psychic and cannot guess at each other's feelings and intentions. As our journey changes shape, meaning, and purpose, so should the language we use to communicate to those we love. It seems so easy, yet is so hard to do for many people. Perhaps we all need to practice actually having purpose-based dialogue and intent listening. I have every confidence that an entire world can be changed with clear communication—heartfelt and honest, clear and meaningful—just like the souls do for us. The souls will never stop talking to us because they know how vitally important it is to hear from them, and they will never stop listening to us, because they know how much there is we need to tell them.

Dear George:

On May 19, 2003, my beautiful daughter Brianna was murdered by her jealous boyfriend in a fit of rage. He took from me the only thing that mattered in this world to me. He was convicted of her murder and has since gone to prison but did not even get close to the sentence he deserved. I have such hate now in my heart, and I feel like it is consuming me. I don't know how to shut it down—how to shut out the pain and the anger. I know you have talked to many families who had a loved one murdered. How do the souls try to help people like us who have a black heart from so much pain and hate?

—Nate

There aren't enough words in any language on the earth to express the terror and pain of losing a child. Even the souls have conceded that it is the most difficult of lessons to endure on the earth. It carries such a potential for disaster to the rest of our existence here that just finishing our journey on the earth as a bereaved parent is the single biggest miracle of faith I can think of. The road of a parent who has lost a child, especially due to a violent passing, is fraught with holes deep enough and dark enough that if you fall in, you may never come out. This is why parents who endured the pain of the loss of a child find such magnificent reward in the hereafter for having hobbled through this existence, trying to maintain even a shred of hope and faith that it will all be better again someday. Here is a fact from the souls: One day you will see your child in a world of joy and peace, and this darkness will seem as if it had never happened. The hereafter has the ability to reunite children with their grieving parents at a point in both their lives where it seems not a second has passed since they last saw each other. It is a gift the bereaved parents receive for their ability to get back up again after collapsing under the weight of one of the hardest experiences for our minds and hearts to comprehend in this lifetime.

I think technology is a wonderful thing, and I wish I understood it a little better. What I do know about e-mails is that they have a time stamp on them, and I have noticed over the years when I do get to see an e-mail, that the most honest and heartfelt e-mails I receive were written in the middle of the night, when despondency eats up the last of our hope. These e-mails are written at an hour when sleep cannot come and pain will not cease. The only counterbalance we have is that the same hour when we feel we are the most alone is when the souls are closest to us on the earth, to bring comfort.

I always find it so remarkable when the souls of children speak to their parents in a session. In a very real way, the roles reverse—the child becomes the caregiver, and the parent becomes a child, struggling to understand and learn. Children tend to speak much slower and more purposefully to their parents in a session, and they often repeat themselves, because they know the words are having trouble sinking in. The children have to walk through a minefield of darkness and anger within their parents, to find that place of love and hope that is still there, no matter how deeply buried by pain. But children are quite resourceful in finding that spot and reawakening hope and peace within their parents. They understand how important it is to the rest of our existence here that they reach that part of us that will continue to move on for the sake of their child, because something within them knows they still have a job to do—to be a fitting parent to a child no matter where that child now lives. So the children speak directly into the hearts of their fragile parents to remind them that no matter how things appear on the earth, they are still the parent of a beautiful child.

The question is: "Where do I go with a heart full of hate?" The answer is both simple and complex—*nowhere.* You cannot continue your journey here in that state, and trying to sleepwalk through the rest of your existence here because your heart can no longer feel will only be the saddest waste of a lifetime. Each of us can and does recover after a tragic loss—*if we want to*—but it requires re-evaluating everything in our lives we thought we knew and could count on. We have to go back and find a way to rekindle faith, hope, belief, and find a way to know for sure that we have not lost anything, despite what we may think otherwise. Instances like these are where the souls, from their own place of real understanding, can be our best allies in the war to find a way to continue living on the earth in love and hope.

So many parents feel helpless and out of control after the loss of a child, especially if it was a violent passing. They feel they have failed their children by not doing enough to protect them, which is a terrible thing for them to burden their hearts with. Each of us, whether we understand it or not, has a day and time we will leave the earth when our journey here is completed, no matter what our physical age, and no matter what the circumstance. We are not in control of that part of our existence, nor should we be. When we have learned everything we were supposed to learn on earth, including impacting the lives of those around us, we graduate from this existence to the joy and peace of the next. The circumstance of our passing is only the means by which we get from this life to the next. How we pass is usually not a lesson for the soul passing, but rather, for those left behind. It's part of our life's work to cope with the loss of a loved one and find a way to understand and accept the difficult circumstances that have come with it. It is part of *our* life lesson, and for good reason. How we pick up the pieces after loss says as much about us and our journey as how we loved those around us, and how we continue to think about them in their new world. What we learn about ourselves and others after the passing of a loved one is one of the most important tests of faith, love, and hope that we can live through on the earth. But we are never alone in the struggle, and we are connected to those we love and lost in the most special of ways. They are with us constantly, helping to dull the pain, helping to provide insights, and helping to rediscover our hope. The souls have never left, so therefore we have never lost a loved one. It's something that's important to consider when you feel everything has been taken from you. In this instance particularly, you are quite mistaken.

I wish I could just snap my fingers, repeat the words of the souls, and everyone would find forgiveness and understanding. It doesn't happen that way, nor should it—reaching our goals in our lessons here requires hard work, or it would not be much of a lesson at all. But each of us knows that for our very survival, we have to find a way to make sense of the senseless and trust that it all will come full circle for us in understanding and peace. This is a promise the souls make to each and every one of us. We just have to meet them half-way and find it within ourselves to start the process of healing—by finding forgiveness of others and ourselves.

One of the best examples I have witnessed to prove how much the souls understand the value of forgiveness came from a session with another couple whose daughter's life was cut short by a jealous boyfriend, who then took his own life. One of the parents' biggest fears was that he was still with her in the hereafter, and still able to torment her. Their daughter quickly put that notion to rest, helping them to understand that the hereafter is a place of joy, peace, and understanding, and that she had forgiven him and was help-ing him to try to find forgiveness for himself, and to be able to learn from his mistakes on the earth. Then she asked for something that stunned her family—she asked them to pray for the boy who took their daughter's life. She asked them to find forgiveness in their hearts and find a way to help him to help himself by sharing their love not only with her, but with him as well. She told them he was trying very hard to fix what he had done and learn from the joy and love of the world hereafter, but that he needed their help to continue to learn and grow. Instances like these are such defining moments in my communication with the souls, because we can get a glimpse into how necessary it is to keep love and peace growing in our own lives, and how anger, resentment, and an unwillingness to forgive have no place in the hereafter, or our world, if we expect to survive loss and the rest of our lives. A murdered girl asks for forgiveness of the boy who killed her, because she has herself already forgiven him and moved on, and the only way she could help her family to heal is to ask them to find a way to forgive him as well. I wish I could tell you that after the session, all was well with this family—it wasn't. They were angry and hurt, and terribly annoyed with me that I dared bring it up and even mention his name. But I had to remind them that if they would do anything for their daughter on the earth, they had to be willing to put their money where their mouths were, and into one of the hardest tests of their lifetime. If they wanted to continue to live, then they had to find a way to forgive this boy and the madness of his actions, and come to terms that he was a sick person on the earth who only now understands and accepts the terrible things he had done. Their daughter had a simple and heartfelt request for them, and it turned their world upside down.

The wheels of understanding and acceptance move slowly, especially after loss, but they do continue to move. I heard from the family again nearly a year after the session. They wrote a note to tell me that they thought long and hard about what their daughter told them in the session, and they felt the best way to honor her life was to *try* to find some compassion in their hearts for the young man who caused them so much pain. They are making progress, slowly, as we all will—if we *try*. I can't promise it will be easy because I know it won't be—there will be lots of back and forth until you make up your mind to honor your child's life in the best way you know how—by letting the anger go, and concentrating on the love you have for her. Do it for the one person who matters—your child. Anything you do to move your soul away from blackness will bring you a step closer to your child every time you try. Your heart still has the capacity to love, because you still love your child. So we know your heart still works. What you do with that love, and how you let it dissolve the hate you feel, will be the road that takes you right back to your child one fine day.

Dear George:

I am a seventeen-year-old girl who once dreamed of being a model but had my life sidetracked by acute myeloid leukemia. It's so hard to look in the mirror now, all I see is a fat, bald girl from my treatments. You know, I used to turn heads at the beach, but now people look at me with pity and it's disgusting. My prognosis is not good and I accept that I don't have much time left. I don't want to seem like I'm bitchy or complaining, but why? Why couldn't this wait until later in my life? My friends are going out, dating, having romances, and I have treatments and medicine and hair falling out and pain and terrible weight gain. I just wish I could have been normal

*a few years longer, cause I won't ever have a boyfriend or
children or a nice life. I know from your other books you
talked to people in my condition who passed on already.
Did they have anything to say that might help me understand?*

—*Keara*

This letter touched me in a way that actually surprised
me. In reading it, it brought to mind my own teenage
years and the pain of not wanting to be different from other
people my age. No matter what I did, I seemed strange to
the people around me, and life became a little lonely because
the differences between me and the rest of the people I knew
my own age just seemed to get bigger and more pointed. I
also tried hard to be "normal" and I wished I could just be an
irresponsible teen with friends to have a burger with, or see
a movie, without the shadow of the souls constantly over my
shoulder. I also knew that physically I was strange and
small—and I would have given anything to look like Errol
Flynn, a movie star who was famous in the 1940s. My insecurity about my physical appearance only made the fact that
I could see and hear the souls even that much more of a reason for people to avoid me, and it hurt. I grew to hate my
ability because it made me different, just as this girl hates the
cancer that is making her something she doesn't want to be.
It happens. We try so hard not to let ourselves get down, but
we try so hard to stand up that we fall down anyway.

This letter is remarkable in that the young author understands her circumstance and has no illusions about it. That says a lot about her level of maturity, and it also makes me feel glad that she understands that while her life on the earth may not be long, this disease is perhaps one of the biggest life lessons she will endure, and having learned it will bring her a lifetime of joy in the hereafter. But we can be brave all we want, and as understanding as we can be, but it doesn't prevent us from falling down a little in our faith and asking simple questions like "Why did this have to happen now?" The answer, as provided by the souls, may surprise you.

Years ago, in a book I wrote called *Walking in the Garden of Souls* I wrote about Jeff Patterson, the young son of Dennis and Pauline Patterson, who passed from acute lymphoblastic leukemia. The cancer found Jeff at a time in his life when the world should have been his oyster, but he also endured painful treatments and had to come to the hard realization that life as he knew it would never be the same. Things went horribly wrong with Jeff during his treatment—his body rejected the bone marrow transplant and his skin began to disintegrate, exposing the nerves underneath his skin. He suffered in a way that no person, young or old, should ever have to suffer. But in that statement, it shows how little we understand about why things have to happen the way they do, and how important the things we endure during our struggles are to our journey here to a world of joy and peace.

When Jeff's parents came for a session, Jeff was back to his happy self in the hereafter, and spoke very matter-of-factly about the intense suffering he endured. "Yes," he remembered somewhat vaguely, "it was terrible," but his next statement astounded both me and his family. He told us that he did not regret his passing at a young age, or his pain and suffering, because it brought with it such reward in the hereafter that he was rather proud he went through it. But he stunned all of us by saying he "would go through every second of the pain again" in order to receive the kind of reward he now enjoys there. That's a big statement, considering that he was sick at a time when he should have been dating, having fun, and just enjoying being young. But here is the extraordinary part—he is doing everything like that and *more* in his new world. Communication from souls like Jeff helps us all to understand that nothing is ever lost to the earth, and everything we ever wanted and couldn't quite have is given back to us in abundance in the joy and peace of the hereafter, when our struggles on the earth have been completed.

I know it may be hard for us to understand now, but sometimes we have to wait for life to get better before we can truly understand how much our struggles contributed to making us the people we will eventually be. What used to make me feel isolated and lonely now makes me feel unique and empowered. And in understanding why I was chosen for this particular life journey, I see the value in having gone through the pain. It brings joy later on, it truly does. It does not matter whether that joy comes here on the earth or in the hereafter, but I can tell you that the souls promise their joy is so complete that they cannot even get us to fully understand—there simply aren't enough words. So we have to trust that perhaps things aren't wonderful right now, but everything we ever wanted will come, and in a time and place we can truly enjoy them—free of pain and sickness, and in a world where we will be young forever.

When I responded to Keara's letter, I told her that I feel like she and I are kindred spirits, and I wanted us to make a promise to each other. We will both wind up in the peace and joy of the hereafter, and I want us to find each other. There, in a perfect world, she will be thin and beautiful, and I will be tall and dashing. We'll sit under a beautiful sky, and laugh about that distant world whose effects we can no longer feel—the pain of growing up different, the worry about our physical appearance, and our new understanding of how little those things actually mattered. We can talk about our accomplishments—keeping a heart full of love despite loneliness, and finding the peace of knowing one day it would all work out for us. None of the silly trifles we worried about will actually matter, in a world that returned to us everything we thought we had lost on the earth. We will have won the battle of illness, shyness, pain, loneliness, and insecurity. Our best life ever will be waiting for us.

CHAPTER FOUR

Things That Go Bump in the Night

Dear George:

Are there really such things as ghosts?

—Dara

A very simple answer for a very simple question—yes. Well, yes and no. Yes, in a very practical way, but no, not in the way most of us have been taught to think. Suddenly, a simple question is no longer that simple. It's no matter—everything within the world of the souls seems to require a lot of explaining, because their world and what we *think* about their world has so much complexity and misinformation that sometimes it's just best to start with a simple question.

Yes, there are ghosts. There are also spirits, angels, beings, ectoplasmic masses, electromagnetic anomalies, and entities. There are even more names that people will create from their limited understanding and poor education about the people who once walked the earth and return to help those of us still here. These are all fancy and sometimes contrived words for the *souls*. When people try to explain things they don't quite understand, it's rather like the parable of the blind men and the elephant—what we think we feel is what we think we see, and because most of us are only able to touch what is in front of us, we do not see the entire picture or understand it. Just like the blind men in the parable, whose limited knowledge was based only on what they thought they had experienced, and since they each had a different experience, not one of them realized they had experienced the same thing. So with regard to the souls, each of us who feels we have experienced them or their world have varying and sometimes conflicting ideas about the souls, and what they can and cannot do.

For most people, their education about the souls and the world hereafter seems to be based mostly on supposition, fear, elements of their religious beliefs, anecdotal stories from others, and factless history. Because the souls cannot often be seen or heard, they have no way of defending themselves from stories that go from the fantastical to just plain strange, and they have no way to counter the terror of the unknown that seems to grip people who fear what they cannot immediately understand.

This seems to begin as early as childhood, where darkness brings fear of things that "go bump in the night"—which seem to have no other rational explanation than something mendacious or evil. Religion is also another huge culprit in perpetuating the notion that we are constantly under attack by things we cannot see. I remember as far back as when I was a student in Our Lady of Perpetual Help School in Lindenhurst, Long Island, listening to the Christmas Story and hearing how when the Angel appeared to the shepherds to tell them about the birth of Jesus, they were frightened. Even as a child, after hearing from the souls myself, the story made no sense at all. Why were they afraid? An angel comes to the earth, bringing with it joy, peace, and hope, and the shepherds could neither feel its joy nor see the beautiful image of peace? It seemed impossible. Knowing the kind of energy the souls bring with them—which is exhilarating—I couldn't fathom for a second that anyone would be afraid of an apparition of joy. But people *are* afraid. They are afraid because they take something beautiful and make it terrible in their minds, because they don't understand enough about the souls and their world to make a valued judgment on just what they are experiencing. I understand that my work affords me a much different perspective on the souls because I can see and hear them, but there are also people on the earth who have seen and heard loved ones who appear for them in visitations that also bring them peace and joy.

Perhaps not enough people have been properly educated, and I know part of my life's work on the earth is to educate more people about the presence of the souls on the earth, and how important it is to us that we accept, honor, and value their appearances, rather than fear them.

Yes, the souls exist, and yes, they are sometimes on the earth. And for a very good reason—they want to help us to continue living our lives here. They are cheerleaders on the sidelines of the often confusing and difficult road each of us is on. And their presence in our lives and on the earth helps us to understand that our goal is to do the best we can in this lifetime, learn from their example, continue forward no matter how hard, and earn the right to go on to a world of peace.

One of the things that irritates me the most when I hear the stories of people and their "ghosts" is the negative context in which it is nearly always framed. There is NO negative context that the souls could *ever* be framed in, because they come with the energy of peace and joy. They come, they visit the earth, they help us when they can, and then they leave to return to their beautiful world. The souls visit, sometimes for our good and sometimes for their own, but they do not live in our world. They live in a far better place than we can imagine, and only a fool would think the world *we* live in is so fine that the souls are all too eager to come back. They aren't. They do what is necessary to help us on the earth, and they return to their world of joy.

What I find interesting in sessions is that although the souls will communicate, they are not always interested in the earth, and for some pretty remarkable reasons. Life here wasn't all that wonderful for them, especially compared to the world they now live in, and some souls who have communicated tell me they will *never* return to the earth—that life here was just too hard for them. They are willing and able to communicate to us, but they prefer to stay away from the confines of this world and the pain and worry that seem to permeate our existence. They have graduated out of all of it, and they prefer the world of joy and peace they now have.

I suppose that it is part of the human condition to see something, not understand it, and create another story for it that will incorporate all our darkest fears and worries about elements of the world whose true meaning eludes us. It's the same reason why roller coasters and fun houses were invented—to give us a reason to feel manufactured fear and uncertainty. It just seems a shame to me that those things are also used to describe the souls, and nearly always by people who have had no actual contact with the souls. Talk to a person who has lost a child, and has seen that child appear for them either in a dream or when they were fully conscious. They will tell you that they were mesmerized by the apparition, and they felt the peace and joy of the souls just as clearly as they could feel their own heartbeat. This type of feeling is indicative of a real appearance by the souls. Whenever I hear fear in the stories of people who claim to have seen the souls, I know it is perhaps part visitation by the souls and the rest is someone's projection of their own fear and insecurity thrust onto what should have been a wonderful, comforting experience.

Yes, there are "ghosts," but that word is a tragically flawed description of the souls who want so much to reach out to us and show us that there is *more* to this lifetime than we can ever imagine, and that their presence should signal a sense of hope that no matter how much we struggle on the earth, we break out of the pain, fear, and uncertainty of this world and move on to a world that defies our understanding of just how wonderful a world of joy and peace can be. The souls only want to help point us in the direction of hope, and to be a beacon they hope we will follow, through our own struggles and on to our reward.

Dear George:

Can you tell me why some places are haunted? Why would a soul stick around and do things that were tied to their lives here, even hundreds of years later? Do they get to choose to do that?

—Carrie

I look upon the word *haunting* the same way I look upon the word *ghost;* I don't like those words because they bring a negative context to a perfectly acceptable and understandable occurrence by the souls. I much prefer the word *visitation*, because it is a much more accurate description of why the souls return to the earth and what their purpose is in the context of our lives on the earth.

Haunting is a rather unflattering word, even for the souls. If I said, "Carrie is visiting me," it would be a fine statement. But if I said, "Carrie is haunting me," it would have a negative and offensive connotation. The souls visit the earth periodically for us, for themselves, or just to help people who are struggling and need direction. People take this to be something terrible or scary when it's not. It's only the souls making a connection with the earth for a very short time. I think perhaps in trying to explain how and why the souls visit the earth, it would be better to take it out of its already overworked context and put it into an everyday context that we on the earth can easily understand.

I still reside on Long Island, New York, not far from the home I grew up in. While it isn't around the corner, it is close enough that I could drive by if I had the time and inclination to see it again. And I certainly have on a few occasions.

When I visit the house, I invariably do the same thing—I get out of the car, walk the crooked cement sidewalk where I used to skip on my way home from grade school, look at the bushes where we used to play hide-and-seek, and look at the door where my mother used to stand, arms crossed, waiting for us to come home for dinner. It may only be a few minutes, but I am able to relive a lifetime of memories there, in that funny little house that looks even smaller each time I visit. When I am feeling nostalgic, a trip to that house to remember both good and bad times seems to do me a world of good.

You have just witnessed evidence of me *haunting* the home I grew up in. I hope the example helps everyone understand how mundane and simple the act of the souls visiting places that were meaningful to them on the earth actually is. There was nothing negative or evil about my visitation to the house. I didn't go to do the present owners any harm, and I certainly didn't go to make myself a burden for the next hundred years. Other than the times the souls visit us to bring comfort or peace to us, sometimes the souls' only interest in visiting a place they knew is because it was part of their memory, which they still value. It really is as simple as that.

The souls find it rather comical that entire enterprises have cropped up to deal with *haunting* and even more hilarious—that we are arrogant enough to think we can hire someone to wave their arms around or shake their trinkets to "remove" the souls, who consist of nothing but electromagnetic energy and cannot make a dent in our physical world. Trust me, we cannot make the souls do anything they do not want to do; we have no control over any aspect of the souls or their world. But the souls are a lot more understanding about our concerns that phenomena around people and houses *do* happen—but the reason why may surprise you, because it actually has nothing to do with the souls.

I met Gary Jansen, a fellow Long Islander and author of

Holy Ghosts—Or How a (Not So) Good Catholic Boy Became a Believer in Things That Go Bump in the Night, about a year ago, after he was kind enough to send me a copy of his book. Gary's book chronicles his evidence of having souls in the home which he considered "earthbound spirits," and the nefarious things Gary seems convinced they had done. I have to admit that I am not a fan of books and shows about the paranormal, mostly because it is a bit of a busman's holiday for me. But I did read Gary's book with interest, because I know Gary lives in a century-old farmhouse—and anything with history in it has my undivided attention.

I must say up front that I find Gary to be very credible and sincere, and I don't doubt for a second he picked up on the phenomena of having souls in the house. There is nothing unusual about that. If there are people who occupy a home, there will occasionally be the souls of friends, loved ones, and previous occupants who will simply drop by for no other reason than to visit us or the home, and move on. But the thing that concerned me about the telling of the story of his "haunting" was the negative connotation attached to what seems clear to me as only an extended visitation by the souls, which actually seemed to have a bigger purpose— perhaps to help resolve some lingering issues within the family. Instead, the souls were considered the cause of them. In fifty years of hearing and seeing the souls, I've never come across an "evil" or "negative" soul—they don't exist, because they now live in a world of peace and joy, regardless of how many times they may visit the earth. Sometimes things like this may just be a matter of perception—because of my work with the souls and a lifelong relationship with them, I could never see their visitations in any other light than a positive one. I know from experience what they are capable of, and more specifically, what they are *not*.

This is what I have learned about houses that are purportedly *haunted*: houses hold energy, both good and bad, and that energy stays, sometimes locked in walls or balled up in corners of houses where both happy and unhappy things occurred. Although there are occasions when happy memories will repeat themselves like a recording—I have a friend who can still hear clearly the sound of her children running through the dining room, even though they are now adults—the majority of energy buildup and replay comes as a result of unhappy times, frustration, sadness, depression, and bad things that happened within the home. It was not surprising to me at all to read that there were problems in Gary's family, and that the negative energy would plant itself and recur when there was more sadness, stress or tough times. Often when we encounter this kind of bad energy, it is ignited by whatever troubles we are feeling at the time, and the projection of our own fears sets it ablaze and sends it everywhere once again. How unfortunate, I thought while reading his book, that it was blamed on the souls, who most likely were only there and hanging around to try to help. To me, that was one of the tragic circumstances of growing up Catholic, believing in fear, and then having your worst fears project themselves onto the very people whose love and concern we could have depended on just by their very presence around us and in our homes.

I've been invited to many, many "haunted" homes, only to find complete peace and the occasional curious soul who seems more curious about *my* interest in the home. Many people are still familiar with the *Amityville Horror* house on Long Island, which I had the opportunity to look at when it came up for sale. I had an interest in the house because it was beautiful and sat right next to the water. The story that accompanied the house held no interest for me whatsoever, because I know from "feeling" the house that the story was not entirely the truth. As the tale goes, there were multiple murders in the house when it was owned by the DeFeo family. It was subsequently bought by the Lutz family, who claim to have encountered "evil spirits" and a "demonic presence," which forced them to flee the house shortly after they bought it. What struck me about the house when I toured it was how *serene* it was—I'm sure the buildup of negative energy, fear, and dread had dissipated long ago, and what was left was a lovely old Dutch Colonial. I decided against buying the house because it would have been my worst nightmare to have so many curiosity-seekers wandering by and snapping photos, but I don't doubt that what the Lutz family may have felt was the lingering fear and dread of so much bottled up energy in the house from when the DeFeo family lived there. Even before the murders, there were rumors of domestic violence, heated arguments, and terrible times, according to accounts from neighbors nearby. Houses hold energy, both good and bad, but the souls hold no ill will to anyone, even if they sense our fear and struggle, and come to help us in any way they can. I find it tragic that they are blamed for something over which they had no control.

It may be interesting for you to know that my home on Long Island has been "haunted" since the day I bought it, and has been for years. When I first moved in, I felt the soul of an old man on the second floor, who seemed to make his way to the bedroom at the far end of the house. Over the next few weeks he "appeared" (at least in a way I could discern because I see the souls) a few times, and acknowledged that he could see me as well as I could see him. I never asked his name, and he never spoke. Later that year, when Halloween came by, I had very few children willing to climb the very steep hill and seemingly endless steps to the top of the hill where the house sits, but one little boy came to the door. Since there were so few visitors, I showered him with more candy than he could find at ten houses, and he looked inside and said, "My grandfather used to live here." I told him that it wasn't likely because the house was newly built, but he insisted he was correct. "The house used to be right over there," and he pointed to the very place the soul of the old man seemed to want to walk—the bedroom at the far end of the house. Now it all made sense. I see the soul every once in a while, but he has no interest in moving in; he just visits occasionally, and I rather like the fact that he comes around. His visits, to me, are comforting and peaceful. Visitors to my house have all, at one time or another, seen my cat BooBoo from twenty-five years ago, still running down the stairs to the kitchen. It used to really scare some people, but now they seem used to it. Again, BooBoo is not a permanent fixture in the house, but he does occasionally visit with me and spend some time, I think, intentionally annoying my present cat, Elton.

Things are not always what they seem, and we have to be careful not to jump to uneducated and simplistic views of the very souls whose spiritual work it is to keep us to our journey here, and provide a constant source of love and peace for us. You can understand why it is so maddening for me to hear people blame a myriad of circumstances (almost always bad) on the souls. The souls' only interest in visiting us is to provide us with some spiritual support when our faith is sagging, and to give us a source of inspiration along our journey. I wish more people would welcome their visits rather than fear their presence. They have so much to teach the world—if we could only get used to not fearing or blaming them for our own failures and fears.

There is an interesting postscript to the story of Gary Jansen's house. I discovered through my assistant that Google has a mapping system that enables people looking for a particular address to see the street and actual house through a series of photographs of each and every individual street and house over most of the country and world. My assistant typed in Gary's address so that we could see one of the few remaining examples of a historic Long Island farmhouse, and Gary's home did indeed pop up. As we looked closer at the photograph one thing became clear: captured in the photograph is the soul of a woman, sitting serenely at the steps of the front door.

Dear George:

What are your thoughts on Ouija boards? I've messed around in the past with friends with interesting results. My mum always used to joke that if she died I should try to contact her and she would respond. Now that she has passed onto the hereafter, I'm wondering if I should try.

—Corinne

I would like to answer Corinne's question. In fact, I would like to talk to her directly. So instead of opening my mouth and communicating, I will simply get out a cardboard table game, call three additional friends to help me, and allow my energy to move a plastic indicator around the board until I can spell out each letter of the words I want to tell her. Of course, I am being facetious, but it is hard for me to answer any questions about things like the Ouija board with a straight face.

Ouija boards rely on the power of suggestion, which scientists have proven to be even more powerful than our conscious thought process. Once again, they operate by tapping into a place within each of us that holds fear and misguided belief in things we don't quite understand. An interesting fact about the game (and it is, after all, a game) is that it was created by Elijah Bond in 1890 strictly as a parlor game, but did not take on any mystical capacities until a woman named Pearl Curran found the game, changed her name to Patience Worth, and decided that the game was an important tool for divination and reaching "the Beyond." From nearly the beginning of the time the game was used as a paranormal accessory, critics, like I. W. Howerth for the *Scientific Monthly*, blasted it as the "vestigial remains of primitive belief systems." I find that characterization of the Ouija board to be very accurate, because it relies on our most basic fear of anything we can't understand and don't actually bother to find out about. People have given it a kind of undeserved credibility by crediting it with the conjuring of "evil spirits" and tapping into the world unseen. To quote my father, "It's all a bunch of hooey." All in all, the Ouija board's appeal seems to be recognized only by children and those with only the most basic of spiritual education.

There is a common misconception about the souls that both the souls and I will spend the rest of my life here trying to clear up. As hard as it may be for us to believe, the souls *do* have better things to do than entertain us. Yes, the souls do and can help us whenever we need it, but the souls closest to us know best when and how to approach us. Souls who do not know us have no reason to contact us, because they have no connection to us unless there is some kind of relationship we share, like when a client comes to a session and the soul must communicate to *me*, a relative stranger, in order to get the messages across to its intended recipient. That is the only time the souls who do not know us will try to communicate to us. The notion of assorted and unrelated souls lining up to communicate with us just for fun is about as preposterous as thinking your favorite movie star is going to call you on the telephone because he or she knows you are a fan. Don't count on it. It's not that we aren't important; it's just that the souls have far better things to do than wait around for us to get the inclination to play a board game in order to hear from them. The souls are also on their own spiritual journey in the hereafter, and although they may visit the earth, they do it for reasons that are clear and meaningful to them and us.

I suppose that the real allure of the Ouija board lies in the fact that people still think it's possible for souls to be "earth-bound" because of something that somehow was left unfinished on the earth. It's not even possible for the souls to have any unfinished business on the earth, because each of us cannot leave the earth until our spiritual lessons, such as they are, are completed. Yet still, people cling to the nonsensical idea that there are souls who supposedly wander the earth in search of some resolution to an old problem they may have had when they were in their physical bodies—as if the answers somehow could not be provided in the world hereafter and by the Infinite Light, where *all* the souls go.

My sincere hope when I answer questions for people is to provide enough practical information in terms we can all understand from an everyday perspective why the things we have *no* problem believing about the souls, yet would never believe about people on the earth, cannot be possible. It's a matter of practicality, and the world of the souls works very much like our world here—the souls live and learn, they visit, they continue helping us just as if they were on the earth, and they encourage us to continue until we can earn the reward of their world. It's a pretty straightforward concept. And, perhaps, a little simple—maybe too simple for people who are looking for danger and fear around every dark corner in their lives. I think that's an issue that is part of *our* life lessons, not the life of the souls. But again, the more we learn about their world, the more we can be clear and unafraid of our own.

Dear George:

I have heard some mediums say that a soul is "stuck" and needs help to cross over. I have then seen them do this little ritual to help the soul to cross. In your writings I get the impression that all is revealed and understood once we pass over. So I was wondering if there is ever a time when a soul does not know that they have passed away from their human form and also is there ever a time

when a soul will need to be helped to the light from people
on the earth plane?

—Debra

We had a bit of a comical moment when this question was read to me by my assistant. She thought that I should say the same thing in a public forum, and then tell people that it required my doing the *chicken dance* to "unstick" their loved ones from this plane. I certainly don't mean any disrespect to the bereaved, or mean to make light of their grief, but we wondered aloud how many of them would have done the dance with me if they didn't realize I was joking.

I think I will always be at a terrible loss as to understand why we people struggling on the earth with barely enough spiritual knowledge to help ourselves, think we have the kind of control or power to alter the life of the souls in any way whatsoever. People do it all the time, especially when it comes to the passing of their loved ones. I hear so many times from people that they thought if only they had made a better decision, or done something different at those final moments of a loved one's life, that somehow they could change the entire world of their loved one. In doing this, we would unwittingly "spare them" their life of joy and peace on the other side. The power is not in our hands, and we do not have the kind of control necessary to alter the life lesson of anyone, except perhaps, and only to a degree, our own. If we understood a little better our reason for being on the earth in the first place, we might understand a little better that the entire reason for living on the earth is to learn and grow so that each of us will be rewarded with the opportunity to live in a world of joy. Trying to change the sequence of events would be rather like trying on the earth to prevent somebody from winning the lottery and experiencing a wonderful life of leisure. We wouldn't even try if we understood even a little bit how magnificent the world hereafter actually is. If we had a little more courage and a lot more faith, we would willingly and gladly send those we love to a life of complete joy. But we often don't understand, and we mostly don't have enough faith to make the decision to send our loved ones off to their reward, rather than to try to hold them to the earth.

I don't know why somebody who purports to be a medium would be so off the mark as to tell somebody that any soul was "stuck" on the earth. No soul is *ever* stuck here. The souls no longer need their physical bodies to survive, and they certainly no longer need the earth to live. They move on to the most beautiful of worlds, where they can come back to help us continue through our struggles in order to achieve the same reward they now enjoy. Just because a soul chooses to come to the earth in a session or to a loved one who is suffering does not mean that they are bound in any way to our existence. A medium who says they are has no actual ability to hear from the souls, and no real idea what the souls are all about.

Again, it's arrogance and lack of information that makes us think we have any control of our planned destiny on the earth, or in the lives of the souls who now have graduated from this existence into the next. The souls understand our world much better than we do, now that they have left it and can see the world in full spectrum. They understand their transition is something they have *earned*—by completing their journey here and moving on to a better world. What do we think we could actually do in order to make things better for a soul who has already personally seen the Infinite Light and has seen their journey and understood their struggles in a way they could have never understood on the earth? The answer is not very much. The souls, however, can do quite a lot for us. Perhaps *we* are the ones "stuck" in our existence where we are not moving well enough to complete our life lessons? What control do we have over anybody on the earth who has stopped on their journey and has become unable to continue? We have no power to fix that, just as we have no power to change what is to be the souls' greatest transition in their lives. We're best off trying to understand and help ourselves to not get stuck by complacency and an inability to move on simply because the struggles get hard. We are the ones who need tending, not our loved ones or any other soul. But the souls can and do help us in any way they can to see our lives here as a project that will have a beginning, an end, and a new beginning when our work on the earth is done. We need to remember to keep to our purpose here, and not to invent problems where there aren't

any. The souls are in much better shape than we realize—
and we will only understand for sure when we find ourselves
graduated from the struggles of the earth to a beautiful life
in the world hereafter, just like those who have gone
before us.

Dear George:

*Two days ago I bought a book about a little boy who goes
to Heaven after having a ruptured appendix. Anyway,
the little boy claims that you MUST have Jesus in your
heart to go to Heaven. Now, here is the thing: I have read
all of your books and I have come to the conclusion that
what you say makes more sense. But, I must say that it
scares me a bit that there are people who have NDEs who
claim Jesus is the only way, or others who claim to have
gone to hell and back. I don't want to be forming the
wrong beliefs and knock myself out of Heaven. So, I must
ask you if you are absolutely sure that Heaven is for
everyone and not just Christians. I mean ABSO-
LUTELY sure? I quit going to church and reading the
Bible a few years back because I trust what you say. Just
don't lead me down the wrong path if you know otherwise.*

—Christy

There are a lot of concerns contained in this letter so I will do my best to try to answer each of them, and hopefully help people understand a little more about both the souls and what they have taught me about the nature of religious beliefs.

Let's start with the first issue about the story of the little boy and the NDE, or Near Death Experience. In order to be clear, I want to explain that *Near Death Experience* is a term used for people who experience physical death for a matter of minutes and find themselves making the transition from this world to the next. There are so many people who have claimed to have experienced one, but the stories they tell are so far afield from the standard that they raise questions in the minds of the scientists and those who study the phenomenon. As much as we would like to believe that every NDE was real, most are not, and the circumstances of their NDE bear out why. Those who experienced fear, dread or worry during their NDE are thought to have had some kind of experience, but not actually one of touching the world hereafter. Researchers know this because in the telling of their story, too much of their thought process, their beliefs, their fears and worries were connected to the experience. That means simply that their consciousness was still activated and not "dead." We cannot think consciously in an altered or clinically dead state, so any intrusion in our NDE that coincides with what we believe, fear or worry about tells researchers that while a compelling story, it was not an actual Near Death Experience.

I thought it was important to illustrate the meaning of an NDE, because something Christy wrote about the little boy immediately leapt off the page at me. I find the little boy's account of his NDE to be tainted by his own thoughts, because of the statement that apparently he was "told" that each of us "MUST have Jesus in your heart to go to Heaven." It is too much a direct reference to his religious beliefs to be credible. I am sure he meant well, truly believes the statement, and perhaps truly believes that he had an NDE, but because it is obvious that his consciousness was involved, the standard pattern of an NDE is just not there. So without even basing my opinion on what I have heard from the souls for more than a half century, I have to dispute this boy's account just by the fact that it doesn't fit the scientific standard in place since the 1970s.

I have also heard people who insist they were shown a vision of "hell" and demons and all kinds of crazy things. Generally these "visions" have been found to be projections of their own mind and fears onto a circumstance that may come close to a clinical death and NDE, but is not an actual NDE. I was raised Roman Catholic in a very strict and devout Catholic family. I wish I could say I am still a devout Catholic, but I cannot. I no longer follow any formal religion, even though I consider myself a man of great faith in the Infinite Light and the souls. The reason why I don't subscribe to any formal religion is that I believe too much of organized religion is *fear based*. If we are not perfect, we are punished. If we don't get in line, we are left out in the cold.

And if we mess up, God has no use for us. I have learned in so many years of speaking to and with the souls that *nothing* could be further from the truth. We are *loved*, like a parent loves a child—unconditionally and unequivocally. There is nothing we could ever do that God or the Infinite Light couldn't understand, accept, and forgive. *Nothing.*

Could you imagine a child taught by his atheist parents that Jesus and God do not exist, then this child passing on and being told, "No, you do not believe in Jesus and you are not welcome in the world hereafter." It's impossible to even comprehend, but this is what some organized religions and people of religious faith want you to believe. Does it even seem possible to you that a merciful, loving God would be that cruel? I don't really think so. To prove this point, I have heard communication from souls who believed in nothing on the earth—they refused to think there was any kind of being that controlled the universe, and that when we die, we turn to dust and blow away. What I find ironic about these souls is when they communicate from the hereafter to their families here, they are *thrilled* to have been proven wrong, and they go on and on about the grace and beauty of the Infinite Light, almost as if they invented it. I find it funny, charming, and heartwarming that they are so glad they were wrong.

I despise any formal religion that teaches things like hate, punishment, retribution or pain if you dare step out of line. More harm has been done on the earth in the name of religion than any act of violence imaginable. But I don't want to appear to be bashing *belief*. Belief in a power greater than our own, which understands everything in our heart and soul, and loves us more than we love ourselves, is something each of us should not only believe, but *count on*. This is the real nature of spiritual belief, and it is the absolute truth, free of fear and worry. The souls have spoken so clearly about the grace and compassion of the Infinite Light that it seems impossible to even consider what some religions have the temerity to call "God's will." Think of how many religions and millions of devout, religious people do not believe in the figure of Jesus because it is not within the framework of their religious teachings? Do you believe that all those people are thrown away by a merciful God? Do you believe those who were never taught about religion are punished for not having learned? The more you think about it in a practical way, I believe that the more it makes sense. At least I hope. God, or the Infinite Light, loves us whether we believe the sky is green, or if Jesus is a savior, or even if we believe nothing at all. It is all part of our journey of self-discovery that makes us the people we are. It's how we live our life, or *try* to, that brings us closer to the grace, peace, and joy of the world hereafter and the Infinite Light. People worry way too much about religion when they should be worrying about how *they* are making the world a better place by their example of hope, caring, understanding, generosity and peace.

Dear George:

I am one of those people who has been taught to believe that anything that has to do with the souls is a plot by the Devil. I don't believe this is true, but I would like to try to gain some understanding on how the afterlife works. I do not believe that you are from the Devil, but I also don't know where you actually fit in the scheme of things. I, myself, have had a few visits from deceased family members who needed to give me a message, and these souls don't scare me, but I am the type of person who has to make it all fit in my head, so to speak. I am seeking the truth and was hoping that you could guide me in the right direction.

—Vivian

Reading this question brought me back to the time I met Dr. Elisabeth Kübler-Ross at her home in Arizona. If you are unfamiliar with Dr. Kübler-Ross, she was a psychiatrist and the author of the groundbreaking book *On Death and Dying*. She revolutionized our understanding of death and dying issues, spirituality, and the transition each of us will make at the end of our journey on the earth. She was a remarkable, if not a little mercurial, woman who did not suffer fools gladly, or waste time on anything she felt was not moving us forward in our thinking about understanding the stages of death or the very act of dying. I had the opportunity to give her a session, which in itself was rather remarkable, since her belief in mediums had waned greatly after she was duped by a charlatan she had worked with many years ago. So, in giving her a session, I knew that if Elisabeth found even an ounce of artifice in the session, I would quickly find myself sitting outside with the trash at the curb.

Her session was very poignant, and I think it moved her because of so many people who had lined up to communicate with her—most of them she didn't even know. But the messages were each the same—souls who were so grateful for her kindness during their period of dying and transition, and souls who were so proud that she gave their death a dignity the world had never seen before. She sat stone-faced through most of the session, but remarkably, she only became emotional once. Within a few minutes of the beginning of the session, I experienced an odd feeling—one I had never felt before.

The volume of souls caught me completely off guard. "There is a crowd, Elisabeth," I told her, my eyes widening as if to try to fit in every soul I was seeing. "A crowd?" she asked. "Well I know many people," she answered flatly. I was incredulous, seeing what was pictured before me. "No, Elisabeth," I told her with a new respect for her. "Not just a crowd, Elisabeth—there are thousands and thousands of souls." She straightened her tiny frame and raised her chin in pride, and I saw her eyes well up with tears. It is a moment in my life and my work that I will never forget.

I mention Dr. Kübler-Ross because she was a woman not about to have any nonsense with regard to what she knew in her research and in her heart to be true. Since the bulk of her work and life was situated in the Deep South, in nearly every television and print interview, she was asked the same question ad nauseam about how what was written in the Bible differed from her beliefs about communication with the dead. She related a story to me about one such interview, showing how her response confounded just about everyone who seemed to worry so greatly about communication with the dead somehow being the "work of the Devil":

> *"Do you believe in Jesus Christ?"* she asked.
> *"Of course I do,"* the interviewer responded.
> *"Do you pray to Jesus Christ?"* she continued.
> *"Every day,"* the interviewer responded.
> *"Do you feel he answers your prayers?"* she asked.
> *"I certainly do,"* the interviewer answered.
> *"Then you, my friend, are communicating with the dead."*

I don't have quite the wit and intellect that Elisabeth possessed, but I do what I can to help people understand a very simple fact by asking them a fairly simple question: If you actually believe that communication is the work of the Devil, why would anyone work this hard just to bring joy, comfort, and peace to people? To me it makes no sense. What would be the good in "duping" people into peace and hope? What would the payoff be? The Devil is supposed to be the antithesis of a loving and merciful God. It would make no sense to me that any evil entity would work so hard to bring a measure of comfort to people who truly need to hear a kind word, or feel a loving thought, or even experience the miracle of communication through a visitation with a loved one passed on. I don't let anybody get away with the sentiment that this must be some kind of evil at play—I want them to *show me how.* I don't have to prove what I do helps bring peace and hope to people; the souls do that every day on their own, with or without me. But now, I want people to prove to me how this could possibly be an instrument of evil, when people find such hope in the words of their loved ones. I have yet to have anybody—and some have tried—show me anything but pure good that comes out of communication with the souls.

Why does Vivian say in her note above that she has experienced communication from loved ones who were able to transmit helpful messages to her but she worries that others are part of a nefarious plan? The answer is actually quite simple—because she knew and loved the souls who communicated to her. There is no fear of an unknown, because these souls are dear to her. Perhaps we need to stop talking in blind, blank concepts like good and evil, and try to fill them with examples. Vivian was fortunate enough to experience the miracle of communication from the other side, but has any entity ever tried to contact her in a way that made her feel unhappy or draw her away from her faith? I don't believe anyone actually has; it just sounds like a plausible concept to those who refuse to understand how much good can actually come out of communication with the souls.

Once again, what we don't understand because we have not personally seen or felt it tends to cause misinformation, fear, and uncertainty in people. What a shame that same inexperience couldn't inspire hope, anticipation, and peace that somewhere, somehow, people just like you have heard from their loved ones and received messages which surely brought you a sense of peace and comfort. It will always be part of the human condition that we fear what we don't understand.

I think it is also important to point out something the souls have told me so many times since I was six years old that the words can tumble out of my mouth without even thinking about them: *There is no hell, except for whatever hell we create on the earth.* And the only evil that exists *anywhere* is found only on the earth. Of course I understand those statements fly in the face of what we are taught in Sunday school or in Catholic School, but the souls who have been here and have been *there* have no reason to tell us anything that is not the absolute truth about our world and theirs. To me, and hopefully others who have been touched by the souls, the information makes perfect sense. The earth is where we experience violence, pain, poverty, fear, and hate. The souls call *this* existence hell because here is where all the pain and heartache is. In the world of the hereafter, there is only peace, joy, and love. The souls prove that nearly every day, with their ability to help us to help ourselves along our difficult journey. Seeing them and hearing from them brings an exhilaration that cannot be produced by wishful thinking. It exists because they exist, and they are hope and love, because they live in a world of hope and love.

My advice to those who want to learn more and dispel the curious things they have been taught is to stand up and fight the things we know are not correct. The truth rings in our heart, and we know the difference between what is truly right and wrong. We can't be afraid of what we don't understand—and that is not a concept that is relegated to spirituality alone. Science and medicine have always had to fight just as hard as spirituality to find the truth among naysayers and those who simply will not listen and choose not to understand anything that is not something they can see with their eyes or feel with their hands. But life is not that simple. Some things are a matter of faith, and we have to trust in our own heart that we can tell the difference between good and evil, and right and wrong. At the end of the day, we can leave it to our faith in order to fully understand.

Dear George:

As a research scientist, I was wondering what your thoughts (or the souls' thoughts) are on the practice of exorcism? This seems to be squarely the domain of Christianity, and I notice that now the Catholic Church seems to have fallen into its practice. I personally find it to be a form of barbarism akin to medieval bloodletting and the cracking open of heads to release spirits, but maybe you can provide some insight I am having trouble seeing. Is there actually any basis in truth about the need for exorcism anywhere in the souls' understanding of the earth?

—Ken

I am very fortunate to have a technology-savvy staff who set up a computer so that I could just push a button, see the screen, and click on a block that would take me to some of my favorite online versions of newspapers from all over the world. I remember a few years ago, while reading the United Kingdom's *Daily Mail*, I was stunned to see an article with the following headline: "Pope's Exorcist Squads Will Wage War on Satan." It seems that the Vatican had approved teaching young priests how to perform exorcisms, apparently because in their view, cases of "demonic possession" were on the rise. The article left me both shocked and saddened.

The souls have been emphatic, for as long as I can remember even hearing from them, that there is simply no evil anywhere but on the earth. They are also quite emphatic in their insistence that there can only be one soul to one body, and that it is *impossible* for two souls to occupy the same body. The notion of some "evil" entity "possessing" someone seems as preposterous a concept to them as it does to most of us. But yet, people who are without any kind of real information about the souls still believe what is handed to them about "evil" without question. I used to find this kind of talk and belief irritating, but now, as I understand more about the nature of these so called "exorcisms" I am ashamed and saddened.

I don't know why anybody in the mental health care field has not tried to challenge religious institutions for what is an extremely barbaric practice against people who are obviously mentally ill. People who believe their behavior has been altered by an "evil entity" are demonstrating clear signs of a dramatic mental and emotional illness. Yet, instead of getting them the treatment they desperately need, they are subjected to cruel treatments, and their mania is given taciturn approval by people who should know better. In the past, experiences of exorcisms seemed remote and rare, but having the Catholic Church put its imprimatur on something so frighteningly wrong makes me ashamed to be a Catholic, if not actually a good one. Something seems to have gone terribly wrong in people's hope and faith, if even the *idea* of a loving God allowing people to suffer in this way, and subjecting them to de facto *torture* seems plausible.

There is a reason why the airwaves, television programs, and books are filled with stories about ghosts, hauntings, evil, and the like—it is because *fear sells*, and peace doesn't. Evil grabs the front page headline, and good finds its place on the back page. Just like at the amusement park, people enjoy having their wits scared out of them, even though there is never any real danger on the rides they think have the potential to kill them. We know for a fact that amusement parks being inherently dangerous is pure nonsense, but we go anyway. The trouble with belief in evil is that people are not educated well enough spiritually to know that it is also just as impossible to experience that kind of danger through entities we cannot see. Just like the amusement park, the inherent danger is pure nonsense, yet people still believe. As I get older, it becomes increasingly more difficult to abide people who continue to perpetuate the silly stereotype of "evil souls," "dark entities" and the ubiquitous "Devil." And to see the Catholic Church try to cash in on the frenzy of fear makes me think that the souls, and all their wonderful, peaceful words, are losing the battle of our consciousness on the earth. Where has our hope and our ability to reason gone, that we are so easily frightened by something we can't see?

It seems so much easier to believe that the souls bring terror than that they bring hope and peace. That is a sad commentary on the state of affairs of our world. And it could not be further from the truth. Maybe it is because our world is becoming more scary and dangerous by the day, that people would rather believe that there is more dark than light. I know from meeting so many people, from different walks of life and parts of the world, that people are *unsettled* everywhere. They are unsettled by a world that is moving too fast for them, and changes that are happening too rapidly, and the decline of things they once counted on as a standard of decency in their lives. We are living in a world full of fear.

What I find remarkable about the souls—almost incomprehensible—is that no matter what nonsense is created around them, tacked to them, or attributed in a negative way to them, they will *never* stop trying to bring us peace and hope. It's the only thing that has been a saving grace in my work, when I have to plod endlessly through questions about evil and danger and fear that frankly should never even have to be asked, from the very same people who tell me they are hoping to hear words of comfort and peace from their loved ones. The souls are so much more patient than I am, and their patience brings me some measure of peace. They know that they must carefully step through the minefield of our insecurities, our fears, and our lack of real information about spirituality in order to get to that place in us that is good, pure, and hopeful. And we all very much have that place in ourselves, no matter how enveloped in our own fears it becomes. The souls continue to reach into our hearts and try to turn the tide away from thoughts of fear and danger, to thoughts of peace and hope. We cannot survive in our journey here thinking that we are in constant danger. We are not. We need to remember that we are working through an often confusing world for the good of our own soul. Each of us has to try to reconnect to that place within us that has hope. Otherwise, the evil that exists only on the earth does indeed win. And we lose our life lesson in the process. The souls understand from having lived here that this is a world gone mad, and that everywhere we look there is the potential for trouble. We seem so well trained to look at the awful side of our lives here. The souls are working hard to change that within each of us. We just need to give them the chance to help us see the world as it is and the goodness that is everywhere. I will never know why it is so much easier to believe in evil than it is to believe in good. But perhaps that is part of my own life lesson here—to know for a fact that a beautiful world exists for us just past this one, and to constantly hear misinformation spread in order to trip people up and move them away from their journey to the light. I hope the souls can continue to touch each of us, and I know they will. They will touch each of us in our own way, and in our own time. But until we know for sure how wrong we were about the very nature of life here, evil will always be easier to believe than good. Perhaps it is within each of our life lessons to understand that concept when we are ready. Until then, we can count on the fact that the souls will continue talking to the earth in ways they hope will forever change our thinking, our values, and our faith. And one day we will be the beneficiaries of all the peace and hope they have tried to instill in each of us. We can only look forward to a tomorrow filled with peace, and try hard to forget a yesterday filled with fear.

CHAPTER FIVE

Turmoil

Dear George:

Almost ten years ago, I attempted suicide. I was in a coma for three days and placed on a ventilator and was very nearly successful. Obviously I survived. I was not in my right mind, and it did feel like a terminal illness of the soul from which I could not recover at the time. I have no "Near Death Experience" to bring me comfort and did not glimpse or feel the love of the Infinite Light. The mental picture that remains is of a door being shut on me. It feels like rejection. And on my bad days, it is easy to feel like even God did not want me.

What I need to know is that there was a reason I was turned away and sent back. From reading your books, I can imagine what your response would be, that there was indeed a plan, a purpose, and lesson that I had yet to

*fulfill. On a good day I can believe that, but the bad days
are harder to turn around now. I try to hold fast to the
belief that what God did He did for my ultimate good,
and all the suffering in this life will benefit me in the hereafter. Otherwise I am left with the disturbing feeling that
I am so worthless that even God did not want me and the
only person who ever truly wanted me is now gone from
this world.*

—*D.*

I am glad that what I have written about the souls' messages
regarding suicide has brought solace to readers. I believe
what the souls have shared about turmoil, and depression
being an illness of the soul, is among the most important
things I have learned from them.

In reading this letter, I immediately thought of my father,
who, as a young man, was nearly killed when two railroad
cars came together unexpectedly and crushed him. As he lay
on the operating table, he found himself already out of his
body, and running through a beautiful field toward something beautiful he saw in the distance, but he was stopped.
Three men dressed in brilliantly white clothes stopped him
and told him he had to go back, that it simply wasn't his
time. He felt all their love and peace, but the words upset
him. They repeated, "Go back, George, you must go back."
The next thing he remembered was waking up after the

operation with a sense of sadness, even though his Near Death Experience was dazzling and beautiful.

He spent many years after that incident wondering why those souls wouldn't allow him to stay. He felt maybe he was not good enough, or spiritual enough, or maybe he hadn't earned it. All he knew was that the beauty and peace of that place was so strong, he wanted to be there again. Years had passed—he married his sweetheart, had four children, seven grandchildren, retired—but the memory of that place never faded. During those years, he came to understand why he was sent back—he had a life and a journey to fulfill, and he had to live through the experiences necessary to fulfill his life lesson on the earth.

This is the same reason you are still here. You are simply not finished, and the Infinite Light loves you too much to shortchange you from your reward, which you will see when you are truly finished with the journey you have been set upon. We are so much like children on the earth. We want what we want, when we want it. But just like with children that we care for, we sometimes have to think for them, and do what is right for them, rather than what they think they want, even though they may find it cruel. The Infinite Light loves you enough to keep you on your path, so that when it is really your time to graduate from the earth, you earn your reward from every second of pain you endured here. This is the single most important thing every soul learns—that everything they suffer through on the earth is rewarded so much—that they have actually told me they would go through all the misery again, just to have a fraction of the peace, love, and beauty that they found on the other side. They also understand that they had to earn it, and in retrospect, found that all their turmoil on the earth was a very small price to pay. It must be beautiful beyond our comprehension if the souls are able to make that compelling a statement.

The souls have told me so many times that we are here to create "Heaven" on the earth, in any way we can, and they tell me that it is through perhaps our worst and most trying experiences that the lessons are the most profound. Our goal is to bring peace and hope to others, in spite of our own pain. It's the most important lesson we will learn on the earth, and the one that brings the most reward in the hereafter.

We must bear the pain of loss and turmoil and still find a way to keep our hope and belief intact. I don't know why, but I do know how important each second of it is to building a castle for ourselves in the hereafter. We do the work here so we can enjoy eternity there—it's something we all have to remind ourselves of every day of our life, until it is our time to graduate from this world. The Infinite Light loves us enough to prevent us from shortchanging ourselves of a beautiful life hereafter.

I hope you understand how important your journey is, not only to yourself, but to those around you who will benefit from your example, and also the souls who are waiting for you in a world of joy. Every day that passes, from now on, is a step closer to your dream. You just need to find the will to hang on to your hope.

Dear George:

I really don't know what I should be writing. Why do I have a strong feeling that we are borne of a very jealous and egoistic God? He wants us to kneel, beg, and pray for mercy.

My husband and I were very happy—everybody commented that we made the perfect couple. People had never seen so much understanding and love in such a young couple. And then God decides that things should change, and I beg for his mercy because I can't think of my life without my husband and I just forget about food, sleep, and my own life. For days I went without even combing my hair. All this time, my husband is suffering and I ask God to give us some more time. Then I ask him to take my life, too, if he can't give him life—then at least we can go together. But no, our suffering doesn't stop— he makes him suffer in I.C.U. for a month and I just stay outside his room and sleep on the floor in the corridor. But the Almighty God is blind to all this and takes him away after exactly a month. And here I am, still suffering—alive, but not living. My life is incomplete and I can't be happy without my husband beside me.

If God exists, then why so much torture? Karma?
Mistakes in a past life? Well I really don't know how
much more he wants us to suffer for whatever it was I did
to earn this bad "KARMA." When will God be satisfied?
We were married for almost three years, and for almost
two of those years life was wonderful, but last year was
full of suffering. In the end we lost. I had promised my
husband that come what may, I would make him fine (I
was relying too much on God to help me) and if I failed,
I'd take my own life. I need some solace.

—Rina

I certainly understand Rina's pain. She is very hurt and
angry, which is understandable when you believe with all
your heart—hope, pray, and fight for an outcome, only to
have your whole world shatter around you, and the only
thing you love taken away. But I have to tell everyone, in all
sincerity, that the God she describes does not exist.

Our problem on the earth is that we just cannot see the
true picture of events in the journey of not only ourselves,
but those we love. To say that your loved one endured suffering and lost the battle is like watching a movie and turning it off in the middle. Just because we don't see the end
does not mean there isn't much, *much* more.

If you had the choice to keep your loved one on the earth
and in pain, or to let him go to a place where he would never
feel pain again, you would gladly let him go, even if it meant

giving up the one you love so much. That is what love does—it makes us think about the welfare of somebody else more than our own. We love people so much that we would gladly send them to their glory, even at the expense of our own happiness. So although the choice is made for us in a circumstance like Rina's, the outcome is still the same—she has to love her husband enough to let him go to a place where he can live in joy and peace, until she has completed her journey here, and can follow him to that wonderful world.

I know it is impossible to understand when your heart is broken, but all of us will endure pain in this lifetime—it is part of our journey, and something we can only understand when it is over, and we are rewarded for our pain. Some pain will be suffering from illness, and other pain will be from losing a loved one to illness. But I have done more than thirty-five thousand sessions, where the souls insist that now that they understand the entire story and see the reward they earned by living on the earth, they would gladly endure it again to gain what they now enjoy in the hereafter. You can't see the end of this movie yet, but it has a very happy ending—we will see all our loved ones again, and when we do, it will be as if the suffering never happened—the joy and peace of reunion is worth all the pain we endure. The souls also say something extraordinary about the pain they suffered on the earth—once they are in the hereafter, they cannot even feel the concept of pain, or even recall how it felt to be in pain. It is an important statement to know when you have had the misfortune and terrible circumstance of having to sit idly by while a loved one suffers. But I hope you can continue on your journey here in good faith, knowing it will only be a matter of time until you see your loved ones again in peace and joy. Trust me and the souls, it will be worth every second of the pain you endure, and have endured, until it happens.

Dear George:

I appreciated very much your chapter on suicide in Lessons from the Light. *My precious daughter Bonnie was not able to find her way out of depression and addiction and ended her life in 1997. I know in my heart that she is now free of pain, but I miss her so much sometimes that my insides ache. I believe you when you write that those who commit suicide are treated very special in Heaven because they are fragile souls—it makes so much sense that God is loving and compassionate. But why are there those who still continue to believe that the souls are stuck in some world between Heaven and Earth, unable to go to God? I buy their books hoping to find peace, and all I find is more fear after reading their thoughts. Please—for me and other grieving survivors of suicide— please set the record straight.*

—Joan

Any book that says that victims of suicide are in some murky place, unable to see or feel the joy of the Infinite Light, will only have value if you throw it in the fireplace and warm yourself for a few minutes while it burns. That is probably the single greatest hallmark of fraud among someone claiming they have mediumistic ability, where there actually is *none*. Anyone who was truly able to hear from the souls would hear the same amazing words that I have over years of hearing from thousands of souls who have been unable to endure the pain of this lifetime, and somehow believed that abandoning the relentless turmoil in their life here was the only option they had in order to simply stop the pain. I used to think those who believed they had mediumistic ability when they actually have none were well meaning, but to use fear and mystery to make up for their shortcomings in their ability, and worse—to lead a parent in pain to believe that their child, who already suffered on the earth, is suffering still, I find unconscionable. It's one of those things we have to be wary of as bereaved people—not just of people who claim to be able to communicate with your loved ones, but anybody who wants to fill your head with nonsense about what they *believe* the souls mean when they talk about those who have passed by their own hand. We don't need to listen to anybody but the souls, who can and will communicate the absolute truth about your loved ones and their new life of understanding and peace, directly into your heart, if you let them.

Anyone who has actually had communication with the souls (not just mediums, but those who have had visitations from their loved ones passed on, or even as a result of a Near Death Experience) knows that the souls come through with so much love, joy, and peace that they actually shine from the light of the hereafter. They are iridescent, filled with understanding, and finally, at peace—peace with themselves, and peace with their choices on the earth. At long last, they understand their pain, their frustration with the earth, and the illness that although it could not be seen or felt by anybody else, had the capacity to be terminal, just like a cancer.

There is no mystery about the hereafter, at least not to the souls who find themselves there after they leave the earth. It is as practical a world as we could imagine it to be, and it also mirrors the earth in a way we can understand. Could you imagine somebody going to the hospital when they were sick and having a doctor tell them to sit in the hallway between the reception desk and the operating room? This is akin to the scenario some who believe they have heard from the souls would have you believe. It does not ring true when you create a similar example on the earth, and it certainly isn't true when you apply that same thinking to the souls and the hereafter, whose compassion and understanding is so far beyond anything we could ever experience on the earth. No soul is ever "stuck," especially when they are in need of help. I don't even know how anybody could believe such a statement, let alone make it. We sometimes have to look beyond what we fear, and go directly to what we *know*. I believe that if you think without your fear, and really listen to the words these so-called mediums are saying they would seem as non-sensical and preposterous to you as they do to me.

The problem is that so many who hear these false statements are in a very vulnerable place. Anyone who has watched a loved one suffer has a vulnerable heart. Which is why I usually try to speak slowly, calmly, and often repeat myself in sessions. Sometimes those who have been beaten down by having to watch a precious loved one leave them, piece by piece, until nothing but a shell remains, which also disappears, just don't quite hear, because their grief and pain is too loud. Regret and guilt over not being able to help seem to ramp up the noise in their head and in their heart. Set aside your worries and listen to the truth as you know it should be.

Just so that there is no misunderstanding, I want to make it clear that there is also no fear in passing—the souls tell me the transition from this world to the next is as easy as walking from one room to another, no matter what the circumstance that brought them there. We are loved by the Infinite Light, and it makes no difference how good, bad or indifferent we were on the earth—that is the nature of unconditional love. A parent does not stop loving a child because they misbehave—you love them all the more, and teach them the difference between right and wrong. That is very much what the hereafter is all about.

Yes, it is true that those who pass from their own actions are treated in a very special way, because the souls in the hereafter recognize that they suffered on the earth, and because of their inner struggle and turmoil, which is like a cancer of the soul, many if not all of those who pass by their own hand were not in their right mind at the time they thought the decision to end their life was a good one. The souls understand completely, now that they are in the hereafter, that perhaps it was not the best decision, but it seemed to be the only way out of their constant turmoil.

Interestingly enough, although the souls acknowledge that with hindsight being twenty-twenty, they should have tried to seek the help they needed on the earth, they are not completely sorry to find themselves in the hereafter. Many have told me and their loved ones here that they have found peace and happiness—sometimes for the first time in their lives—in their new world. They are treated with dignity, respect, compassion, and love, and they continue to learn and grow in a way that they never could have done on the earth. Even though they acknowledge that they are sorry to have brought such pain and hurt to the loved ones they left behind on the earth, they will concede that their passing was only a matter of sheer *survival*. They wanted to live, but they could not do it on the earth.

Very often in a session with a soul who ended his or her life, the figure of Christ appears behind them—not as an advertisement for Christianity, but because Christ is a special friend and patron to those who pass under turmoil. He brings with him a peace that helps to heal souls that felt tortured on the earth, so that they can continue, in the hereafter, the journey they could no longer walk on the earth. The souls acknowledge that on the earth they suffered from a kind of illness that made them blind to hope and the possibility of continuing. You have to imagine how terrible a circumstance must be if ending your own life sounds like a good idea.

Although we are left with the pieces of a shattered life and the pain of loss, the souls acknowledge that part of their experience, and even their passing, is part of our own spiritual journey on the earth—to walk the road of one who is bereaved, and to try to continue to live in hope. They do concede that it is one of the hardest lessons to learn on the earth. But the souls also continue to communicate to us, in order to teach us *how* to continue on in spite of the heartache and pain. They stay with us, and they become part of our journey on the earth, helping us to help ourselves as we continue through our struggles. These souls become the most vigorous cheerleaders in our lives in order to help us continue.

All of the souls who pass through suicide have told me that they now live in a world of peace—*every single one*. They continue to live, to learn, and to understand their lives in a way that never seemed to make sense to them on the earth. And as part of their continuing education in the hereafter, they spend part of their time in service to people on the earth who are also struggling with turmoil—to help them perhaps hang on one more day, or to seek the help they need, or even to make them understand that they are not alone in their struggles. The souls also help their families to heal, to cope, and to understand that no matter what we think, we could not stop a soul from entering the hereafter if it was their choice to go. If a loved one of yours has passed by their own hand, remember that he or she has finally found peace and continues to guide your life from a special place in the hereafter. If anybody or anything tells you differently, then it is not worth your time or attention.

Dear George:

I have a fear of dying. I have PTSD and have been obsessing about death, ever since I came back from Desert Storm. I lost my brother (my best friend) last September. I almost lost my daughter in April. All of this has really taken a toll on me.

—Kevin

My first experience with war veterans came via my own father, who fought in World War II. When I was a kid, my father would almost never speak about his time in the service, with the exception of the occasional joke to my mother when he saw her wanting to ration the milk we drank or the bread we ate—a holdover from wartime where people had to do without, and if they were lucky enough to even get it, to make whatever they had last longer. Seeing this would irritate my father to no end, and he would pick up the milk bottle, fill the previously poured quarter glass of milk to the top, and say, "Wake up, Eleanor, the war's over, for Christ's sake."

But comedy aside, my brother and I, both history buffs, would try to corner my father and get him to tell us about his time in the service, to try to glean a little more information about what he saw, what he experienced, and what he learned. The same thing usually happened. My father would begin by naming some of his best buddies in the service and some of the pranks they pulled. He'd talk about his service as an Airman in Roosevelt Field on Long Island, and the many friends he knew who went off to combat in the Pacific Rim after the bombing of Pearl Harbor in December of 1941. But when we pressed on about the actual combat, he would look past us, his eyes so far away, and his face would darken. "We lost a lot of good boys," he would say, wistfully. "Good, fine boys." It wasn't until many years later, when I was able to coax my father into sitting for a session that more of the story started to piece itself together through the souls who made an appearance.

Names like Sammy Boy would come through, and within seconds his eyes would light up. "Sammy Boy—yeah, Sam. Good kid," he would say, his eyes suddenly in the past. Or Davey, who came through to tell my father he was walking just fine, after having lost a leg in combat. "How do you like that," he'd respond, smiling faintly. But it was the soul of Johnny—who came through and called out to my father as "Andy," his nickname, since his last name was Anderson—

who made my father's stoic expression begin to melt into his hands. Johnny only wanted to say, "Thank you," and "there was nothing you could do," and with those words, I saw something happen that I had never witnessed in the previous twenty-two years knowing my father. I watched him cry. Johnny was somebody special to my father. He was mortally wounded in combat, by shrapnel that should have hit another soldier, since they had changed positions during the incursion. When Johnny was hit, there was nothing anyone could do but hold him and tell him to hang on as the life slowly poured out of him. I have to admit that seeing my father cry made me a little scared, but I just sat motionless and tried not to look at him, feeling like he deserved the dignity of not having someone witness his weakness. But he quickly composed himself, wiped his eyes and mouth with the handkerchief he always kept in his left pants pocket, sniffed, and smiled. "That Johnny," he mused, recovering, and then smiling weakly. "He was something else."

The session changed my father in a measurable way, for a few reasons. Firstly, I don't think he ever really bought completely that I communicate with the souls—at least not to the degree he did after that session. But also, the guilt he felt over Johnny, and the sorrow at a young life ending in his arms, haunted my father's thoughts for many years.

It's sometimes very hard for us as civilians to completely understand how terrible war and combat can be, because many who return home do not want to talk about it. *Ever.* Sure, we see the movies, we watch the documentaries, but they don't tell us the story of being so scared out of your mind and watching death rain all around you, and having to decide which was better—having died on the field, or having lived with the guilt of returning home when so many didn't.

PTSD, post-traumatic stress disorder, is a fairly new name for a very old condition. It causes anxiety, depression, and physical illness. It comes from living too long on the razor-thin edge of life and death, where staying alive seems as random and fickle as a roll of the dice. Because of my work with the souls, and understanding how mental turmoil brings with it such powerful and life-changing issues, I often have a bone to pick with the medical community. Emotional and mental anguish are *illnesses*. They hurt just like physical illnesses, and just like cancer, can often be terminal. Terminal, because with no other way to stop the pain, many who are experiencing severe emotional illness begin to look for ways to fix the pain—often through drug abuse, alcoholism, and as far as ending their lives just to stop the pain. It's as serious and devastating as any physical condition, and perhaps *more so*, and just because it does not show up on an X-ray or in a CAT scan, it does not mean that it isn't very real for those who find themselves in a nightmare they cannot wake from.

Sometimes I think the souls are at their most compassionate when they speak to people suffering from emotional illness, and some of the most poignant messages come from the souls who lived on the earth with mental and emotional issues. They understand now, in a way that most of us can't even guess, how thick the cloud of fear, pain and uncertainty can envelop someone who cannot find their way out of the grip of turmoil. One of the things the souls have helped me understand is that most of the time it's not quite the loss of life we may have experienced that sends us into an emotional tailspin, it's actually the lack of control we begin to feel—that life is not ours to manage, and that at any moment, we, or those we care about, could disappear in a flash. Most of us don't contemplate our own passing every day, but when people see too much of how fragile the balance of life actually is, either in wartime, or because of the news reports of natural disasters, people begin to feel insignificant and unimportant. It is bad enough when we ponder our own life and death, but somehow this becomes magnified many times when we begin to worry about the fragility of the lives of those we truly care about.

There is a reason you are still on the earth. It is simply not your time to leave. No matter how random death seems to be sometimes, nobody leaves the earth if it is not their time. Even those who have cut short their own journey on the earth have hinted in sessions that there was *something* inside them that told them to *come home.* There is a simple reason for all of this: We have work to continue on the earth, and part of the experience of our life lessons here is perhaps to come so close to the gates of death that we can see through them, but it is not the time to pass through. Part of the lesson involves understanding in a very powerful way just how fragile the balance of life is on the earth, and that we cannot be spectators in our own lives, like watching a parade pass in a comfortable lawn chair. We have work to do, and perhaps the understanding that it could all vanish inexplicably is the small fire that keeps us moving forward—to do the things we need to do for ourselves and those around us, but also, to impact the world with the story of our lives.

Just as it is clear to me that Kevin's brother, and those he saw die in combat, had a day and time that they were scheduled to leave the earth, it is also just as clear that Kevin and his daughter are still here for a purpose. Perhaps that purpose is something he needs to think about. But I see at least one purpose with which I believe he could change the world. Perhaps it is his purpose in life to help others with PTSD, and perhaps the world at large, to understand and accept that emotional trauma is *not* just "in your head," and that it is very real, very painful, and very important. Perhaps Kevin's goal on the earth is both to draw attention to an often misunderstood and misdiagnosed condition, and to honor those brave soldiers all over the world who continue to struggle in silence, and quietly carry their pain.

Just remember, *It does get better.*

We get better at understanding and identifying our troubles, and the more we work toward wellness, the easier it will get. The souls know now that once we return to the world hereafter, the clouds disappear. Even if it has been so long under the clouds that we have actually forgotten what a brilliant blue sky looks like, we can find some peace and a sense of purpose in helping others identify and cope with their turmoil as well. It *does* get better, the souls promise, and they ask us not to be guilty for finding ourselves still on the earth when others have disappeared. There is a reason—you've been called for duty to others who can understand and relate to you and your issues. The real work lies ahead of you in your struggle, but knowing you are not alone, and also helping those who have lost their ability to see clearly, will bring you understanding, a sense of purpose, and hopefully also—a little peace.

Dear George:

It may seem a bit odd to receive a letter from a Catholic priest, but I have been following your career for years, after I heard Monsignor Thomas Hartman talk about you and the comfort you brought many grieving families in his care. I'm not writing to you because of any specific loss, although I do have my fair share of those I love who have now entered the Kingdom of Heaven. I am writing for a personal reason. It seems, after thirty years ministering to the community, that I am having a crisis of faith. I firmly believe in God, but after seeing so much suffering of truly good people on the earth, it has badly shaken my faith that the promise of eternal life may not be worth all the pain and anguish each of us goes through. I feel I have no more answers for people when they look at me and ask why God allows such misery to happen—to children, to

defenseless animals, to the elderly and infirm. I feel like I
have lost my hope. Do the souls believe it is possible to run
out of faith before we run out of time on the earth?

—Patrick

People who are caregivers, whether they are parents, teachers or those in the medical, social, and spiritual fields, do so with a natural ability that seems to bubble up within them like a never ending wellspring. They are counted on every day to find a way to be positive, inspire hope, provide courage, and to help others see possibilities they perhaps couldn't see on their own. In providing so many with much needed reassurance, those who give of themselves to bring comfort and hope to others are among the most generous of heart and soul on the earth. But there is a danger in giving so much of yourself to others. At some point, if there is no way for that well within you to replenish itself—it has the potential to run dry. Worst yet, we don't even see it coming until we come to the point where we try to drink from our own vessel of hope, only to find it empty.

One of the things the souls understand so well, after living on the earth, is the power of hope and faith. They also know, however, that hope and faith can be fragile and easily lost. Many of the souls came to a point in their own lives here where the faith they had in abundance failed them at some of the most critical times in their own lives. These times came when they experienced loss of a loved one, the loss of direction on their journey, or the inability to make sense of a world where there were too many questions, and simply not enough real answers. Some of the most interesting souls to hear from in sessions are the saints—people who were just like you and me, but for their extraordinary faith in God, the world around them, and the goodness they knew was inherent in all people. But because they were human on the earth, they also had a crisis of faith—a time in their own steadfast journey where they could not clearly see the road before them. What made them truly extraordinary is that somehow they pushed on, and pushed with every ounce of their being to force the dry well to produce hope and faith again. And they succeeded. They succeeded because they learned the secret of humanity: No matter how dry the well runs, there is water hidden just below the surface, where nobody can see it, just waiting to bubble up again.

One of the most amazing and poignant things I ever came to learn was found in the personal letters of Agnes Gonxha Bojaxhiu—Mother Teresa of Calcutta. She spent her life ministering to the poor, sick, and orphaned of the streets in Calcutta, India, and worked tirelessly bringing the world's attention to those who often could not speak for themselves. She knew at the age of twelve that she was called to religious life, and then later in her ministry, felt she had a second "call within a call" after visiting Calcutta and seeing the desperately poor, the elderly, and the orphaned children who were starving in the streets, with no way to care for themselves. She quickly set up residence and a ministry in Calcutta, saying, "I was to leave the convent and help the poor while living among them. It was an order. To fail would have been to break the faith."

Most of us know or have heard about Mother Teresa's incredible ministry, and her tireless devotion to God and the destitute of Calcutta, but few people know that she also experienced a profound crisis of faith, where she began to question the very reason of her existence on the earth, where she "felt no presence of God whatsoever" in the unrelenting suffering of the poor, and especially the children. In a personal letter, she wrote:

Where is my faith? Even deep down . . . there is nothing but emptiness and darkness . . . If there be God—please forgive me. When I try to raise my thoughts to Heaven, there is such convicting emptiness that those very thoughts return like sharp knives and hurt my very soul . . . How painful is this unknown pain—I have no Faith. Repulsed, empty, no faith, no love, no zeal . . . What do I labor for? If there be no God, there can be no soul. If there be no soul then, Jesus, You also are not true.

Many people who read the personal letters of Mother Teresa were shocked at the revelation that she also doubted her faith and the existence of God in a world gone mad. But to me, her questioning of everything she believed in is further proof of her extraordinary faith. It was so real to her, so fathomable, that if it slipped even a little bit, it would leave a noticeable emptiness in her soul. The sheer honesty of her statement is proof that she loved God with all her heart, and like a child demanding answers from her parent, became restless with her inability to understand the plan God had for her and those to whom she ministered.

Although Mother Teresa is hardly the only one of the extraordinary who suffered a sagging in her faith, she is the most recognizable because we have seen her, we have seen her work, and she is not just an image on a page of an old, dusty Catholic book. I find her story amazing, because she is the embodiment of all of us who look skyward and say, "Why? Why must things be the way they are?" The souls now have that answer—they now understand why everything happens on the earth the way it does, and they now understand that the question all along was not *Why?* but *What? What is it we are supposed to be learning from the heartache and desperation we see all around us?* While the souls can't share the entire answer with us, because part of our journey here is to figure that out on our own, they can provide us with an interesting concept that I think explains our own crisis of faith in a very clear way—it is not that you no longer believe in God, but rather that you no longer believe in yourself.

The souls tell me all the time that while our belief in a power greater than our own is wonderful and necessary, our belief in ourselves is among the most important lessons we learn on the earth. We don't fail God when we turn away, unable to finish what we started—we fail ourselves. In times when this happens, we need to stop and re-evaluate everything in our journey that has brought us to this point in the crossroads, and understand that the only real complication is which way to continue. The answer, the souls tell us, is actually rather simple—we go in the direction our hearts tell us. We summon the courage to continue, in spite of not being exactly sure where we are walking. Then we summon the interest to follow the road up ahead just a little farther, then we summon the fortitude to continue what we know needs to be done in order to fulfill us as individuals, and our life lesson. Once we begin walking again, we cannot look back to what we lost—we can only walk forward to what we know we must find. And when we walk, we find that the faith and hope we thought disappeared had actually never really left us—it was only hidden under fear, insecurity, and a loss of purpose. We dip our hand in the well and realize there was water there all along—we just were not capable of feeling it.

I am sure we can already begin to see the reasons to continue on our journey, and I hope that even if we can't always see or feel the water in our well, we trust that it will always be there for others to see and feel. This is our faith: We may not always believe in ourselves, but we will never stop believing that to do good things for another in need is to see the face of God in everyone we help by sharing even the smallest bit of faith that still remains in our hearts.

Dear George:

Do we ever really recover from the pain and trauma we experience as children? Sometimes I feel like my life is doomed to be a broken record of love, mistrust, and running away from the people I care about the most. As soon as I get close to someone, my fear of being found out to be a "sham" of a human being makes me put up a wall and force them to leave. I have done this now in several relationships and I now fear that I will never be free of the pain. When I was twelve years old, my mother died, and I was raised by my father. He was always a rather unstable man, but when my mother died he went off the deep end completely. I frequently had to miss school to take care of him and the house; he could no longer work because he had become an alcoholic, and he started to beat me regularly. Then, when I didn't think it could get any worse, the sexual assaults started to happen when he got drunk. Even though I ran away from home later on, and he died from liver cancer, I feel like I am still running away. I have met a wonderful man who I love deeply, but I keep running away from him, and now I fear I will lose him forever. How do I stop myself from ruining my own life with my own actions? I pray that the souls might have some answers for me, because I don't want to keep living this way. It is torture. I want to be loved, and I want to love again.

—Patsy

I hear stories of people and especially children who have passed on every day, and it doesn't take an emotional toll on me, because I know in my heart that the hereafter is a far better place than the earth, and those who find themselves there are the luckiest people in the universe. I don't worry for the families either, because I know that in the blink of an eye, all their pain of loss will disappear one day, when they see their loved ones again. So I can do sessions, even hearing terrible tragedies, with a level head, for which I am always grateful to the souls.

But when I am in session, or even just talking to people, and I hear stories where children were made to suffer and experienced terror and pain, it brings me to my knees emotionally, and I feel the pain of whatever that child, no matter what age they are now, felt at the time of their own misery. Perhaps it is because my own childhood was filled with fear and pain from those who did not understand me, and perhaps it's because I know what it feels to be trapped as a child with no one's help. But I suffer the stories of people who were abused as children almost as much as the children suffered through it. I always feel a special bond with people who experienced an unhappy childhood, and I think it is one saving grace on the earth that a part of my heart will always bleed for children facing turmoil and pain. The souls have told me many times that our empathy is what makes us human, and our frailty is what makes us beautiful to them.

The souls have told me throughout my life that everything we go through is necessary to our journey on the earth. No matter how terrible, *everything* we live through, and learn from, has a reason. But there is a catch in that statement—not only do we have to live through it, but we are required to *learn* from it. If we do not learn from it, it has not been a life lesson, and we cannot fully experience the value of it on the earth, or the reward for having lived through it once we find ourselves in the hereafter. The souls make it very clear that just because we lived through something does not mean it holds any value for us either here or hereafter—we must *learn* from it, and our own mistakes in the wake of it, in order for us to consider it a value to our spiritual journey here.

Children are purest of heart on the earth, because they are the closest to the world hereafter and the Infinite Light, by virtue of the fact that they have just come to the earth not too long ago. So children are full of hope and light, until something comes along to diminish that hope and light. Adults who hurt children are *predators*, no matter what the circumstance. And they are the worst kind of predators. In the animal kingdom, predators stalk and kill their prey as a matter of survival and nothing else. Adults prey on children for the most selfish and depraved of reasons—because they have lost their own hope and light, and they wish to steal it from the easiest target and most hope-filled people they can take it from—children. But adults like this do far more damage than even they realize, until they see the horror of their actions when they witness their own life review in the hereafter. In stealing a child's hope, they also take away the one thing necessary to be a child—*innocence*.

Although I certainly feel the pain and I understand the problem, to only sympathize and understand is not actually helping. For that, I have to go directly to what the souls have told me: No matter what has been taken from us, no matter how badly we want to hide from our past, it will be necessary at some point to face our fears and begin to take responsibility for the rest of our journey here. It sounds cruel and not terribly sympathetic, but there is a poetry in what they are trying to tell us. *Tough love* is tough, but it is still love, and the souls need us to face what we fear the most, until we no longer fear it. Once we get past the fear that debilitates us and prevents us from moving forward, only then can we experience the life we wish we can have.

There is an interesting statement the souls use when it comes up in a session about any kind of sexual assault—no matter what happens to our physical body, no one can ever touch the *you* that is within you. Somebody can damage your body, but they can *never* damage your soul. Souls are perfect, and they remain so throughout the very bumpy road of our lifetime here, and once stripped of the body which enveloped it on the earth, the soul emerges again, perfect, like a chrysalis from a cocoon. It is an important thing to remember when we feel that we cannot recover from the pain of the past, or fix what has been broken by others. We can go right back into our own souls and begin the healing process from the inside out. Our souls still carry the place where the Infinite Light radiates, like a tiny beacon, and we can draw from that energy to rebuild what has been damaged by others. The only wild card here is our own will—we need to truly *want* to change the things that are not working in our lives, and wanting to change takes a lot of work and courage.

Every so often we get to see the help from the souls in a very real and material way on the earth. They do things here to help us understand that we are never alone in our struggles. I read Patsy's letter very carefully, and when I came to the part where she mentioned a sweetheart who seems to be sticking by her in spite of her inability to let him into her heart, I found it heartwarming and actually quite inspiring. It is proof that the souls have been whispering to *both* of them at the same time—to Patsy, to allow her to feel again, and to her sweetheart, for him to be patient while she works out the issues she needs to confront.

If we all look at our lives, we will probably notice that it is no coincidence that the one who truly loves us is the one who has probably taken the brunt of our inability to let go of the past. We may run, but the one who loves us certainly hasn't. My best guess would be that the souls have brought them both together to learn something very valuable, both about trust and patience. My grandmother had an expression for this kind of union: *For every kettle there is a lid.*

We are not doomed to repeat the past like a broken record if we choose not to. But we do have to *choose*. We need to choose what we truly want over what is easy to do, and we have to choose to let somebody in and help them to understand our pain. It's not easy, but so few lessons on the earth actually are. This may not be quite easy, but it is the best thing that we will ever be able to do for ourselves—to allow ourselves to love again.

I hope Patsy will sit down with her beloved and tell him the entire story that she told me. Everything. She needs to cry when it comes, and allow him to cry as well at the thought of anybody hurting her, and his inability to be there in the past to stop the pain for her. After that is done, she needs to set about taking the past out of her heart. It doesn't belong there. We can keep our pain in our head, because it is a part of our lesson here, but there is no reason to clutter our heart with the past. We have to open up some room in our heart for some-one to take up residence there, and not get frightened when we see the moving boxes. People with a lot to bring with them intend to stay for a long time. I have no doubt at all that the souls have been working extra hard to help Patsy move on past the pain and hurt, but it is also her responsibility to pick up where they must leave off, and carry the ball herself. It sounds like she is ready, and I have faith in her.

CHAPTER SIX

Finding Our Way Back

Dear George:

It's been days since I have thought about writing to you in the hopes that perhaps the spirits would have some direction for me after a terrible ordeal I and my family encountered on Boxing Day [December 26] 2004. Of course, I am speaking of the tsunami that hit Patong Beach in Phuket, Thailand.

At the time, I was a journalist in the U.K., and my husband, eleven-year-old daughter, and I went on holiday to Patong Beach, which is a gorgeous, idyllic locale. I had trouble sleeping that morning, because I felt sure that we were experiencing tremors, although neither my husband nor daughter felt anything (perhaps because they were fast asleep). I felt something was amiss, but quickly brushed that thought from my head as we made our way to breakfast.

Once back in the room, and changing to go to the beach, we heard shouts and noise coming from the beach below our room. We thought perhaps there was a fight starting, but then quickly noticed the frenzied movement of people running in different directions. What I saw next is something I don't believe a lifetime will ever make me forget—the water. The beach tide suddenly disappeared, and I stood transfixed at the odd site of the water seemingly gone. When I heard more shouting, I looked at the horizon to see a wall of water—it moved slowly toward the shore from afar, and I became hypnotized by the sight. My husband was the first to react, as we realized a tidal wave was coming to the shore. We ran to the roof of the hotel where we stayed and could only stand and watch the horror unfold.

Words cannot describe the devastation we witnessed that day. There was an explosion of water, and it just kept rising and moving relentlessly, covering people, cars, businesses, and everything in its wake. People being injured and killed, the utter devastation and debris everywhere, and seeing the desperation on the faces of people whose loved ones were missing became our surreal world. Before we could leave Phuket, we were witness to scores of dead and injured people, and a world gone upside down. It was an experience that still causes me nights of sleeplessness and sickness and worry.

*I understand that I have already written too much,
but I did have a question I hope you or the spirits will
have an answer to. Because of what I and my family witnessed, I am unable to continue my life the same way—I
feel like the devastation has taken away my ability to see
the world without fear and dread. I have since left my job,
because I was no longer able to be objective in reporting,
and I seem to have trouble keeping my composure during
even the most simple of human stories. I feel like I have
lost my life, George. What can I do to find it again? Perhaps the spirits know?*

—Evelyn

There are no easy answers to these questions, but I am a big believer that when there aren't any easy answers to be had, perhaps it is best that we look instead toward understanding—not just understanding of our own issues, but understanding in a different way the circumstances that create the problems we face.

I don't believe there has been one catastrophe in the last forty years that has happened somewhere on the earth where I have not heard from either one of the people who lived through it or one of the souls who passed from it. That list includes nearly every airline disaster, the earthquakes in Italy and Chile, the devastation in Japan, the attack on the World Trade Center towers, Hurricane Katrina, and of course, the tsunami. I've learned a lot from the people who lived through each of these terrible circumstances, the families who have lost loved ones, and even the souls themselves, who each have a different take on the circumstance, and who each find their own way to deal with what they experienced. There are actually two different lines of thinking among those who lived and those who passed, and I think learning about the differences of understanding between them may help all of us find a new way to think about the tragedies we live through, and how to begin coping, understanding, and finding perspective again.

Natural and man-made disasters bring humanity to its knees harder than any other circumstance I can think of. Whether we are directly affected or not, each of us suffers a sense of loss of control, feelings of vulnerability, a frightening reminder of our own mortality, and worst of all—guilt. In speaking to survivors of these disasters, there is an overwhelming sense of *guilt*—guilt that there wasn't more they could do to help, and more profoundly, guilt that they did the unthinkable: They *survived*. It's often heartbreaking to see the shame survivors saddle themselves with, simply because it was not their time to pass, and their lives were spared. The guilt seems to settle in months and sometimes years after healing from the shock and grief of whatever they lived through, and the effects of guilt over not passing like so many who did has the potential to destroy those who survived, if they don't begin a process of understanding and learning, particularly from the souls, how these things happen, what causes some to pass on and some to live, and *why*.

The souls who did pass in these disasters are much more understanding and forgiving of the circumstances than those who actually survived. Firstly, and most important, they understood that it was, in fact, their time to pass. It makes no difference the kind of circumstance we pass in, or the amount of people who pass alongside us—when it is our time to leave the earth, because we have learned all we can here, we continue past this lifetime to the world hereafter. One of the things that is striking about the messages from the souls who passed in many of these disasters is that there was a beautiful sense of community and even *belonging* as they found themselves part of a group of people scheduled to pass together, and in an unbelievable circumstance. Many have told me that while they may have been initially afraid, knowing that they were not alone in their passing made a big difference. In sessions where someone has passed in this kind of circumstance, many names will come through that family members will not recognize initially or perhaps not at all. This is because the souls will rattle off the names of people—most just strangers to them—who at the last moments of their lives became the best of friends. It seems odd to think that the souls would think of complete strangers who also passed with them as dear friends and comrades, but it often brings such comfort to family members to know that their loved ones passed among friends—whether they were longtime friends, or friends joined by the catastrophe they faced. Many souls have gone as far as calling those they perished with their *second family*—hoping to help those who did survive to understand that at the time of their passing, they were comforted, at peace, and *loved*.

It also should be pointed out that the souls who passed on in disasters that became famous around the world actually do understand their place in history. They know that their names will be forever linked with what happened, and to them, there is a kind of beauty in knowing that perhaps their passing has taught the world something about compassion, coming together in times of need, and finding ways to prevent disasters of the same kind in the future. It should be pointed out that there has never been any vitriol or hatred on the part of the souls, especially to those who may have been directly or indirectly responsible for their passing. There is just understanding and peace. It seems the souls know something we don't, but they do know that it is something we can learn—*faith*.

One of the most poignant stories to come out of a session was from a soul whose family came to see me a few years after September 11, 2001. It was a particularly difficult session, because the family witnessed footage of their loved one jumping to his death on that terrible day, when the World Trade Center towers were bombed. During the session, the soul explained to me that his family was devastated by what they saw—his apparent suicide—and that by being devoutly Catholic, they were both devastated and ashamed that a man of such faith would choose to jump, rather than wait to die. "But I had faith," the soul explained. "I had faith that God would save me if I jumped to escape the fire. And he did. He saved me, and brought me to a place where smoke and fire could never hurt me again."

I must admit that it takes a lot to strike me silent in a session, but the sheer beauty of this man's complete faith and belief is something that had a tremendous effect on me. I wish more people would understand how important our faith is to everything we experience, and everything we know to be true. It does not have to be faith in religion or a higher power, but faith in *ourselves* is the most important thing we can learn, especially when we face life-changing circumstances.

When our faith leaves us after a tragedy, we have trouble relating to the world around us. We need to use our faith to find our way back from the pain and devastation we experienced, and we need to rediscover the faith that brought us this far in life. There is a reason why we are still on the earth. We have survived and we need to find the faith that tells us that we were chosen, along with the others who survived, to help people understand what humanity means in a disaster and how it galvanizes people to reach out and help each other not only in the midst of turmoil, but perhaps in everyday life as well. In a disaster, we are no longer people with different backgrounds and social strata—we are a family bound by a common circumstance, and we live together or we pass together, but we do it *together*. We live or die the way the world hereafter has intended us to all along—a community of souls looking for the common good. We find faith and strength, but often at the most terrible times of our lives. Were that we were able to create faith and strength without the disaster, and that is exactly where people like Evelyn come in. She has been entrusted to teach people that we are a community of beings, and what affects one of us affects all of us. I hope she can take her faith, her newfound understanding, and a new sense of purpose, and help teach the world what she learned that fateful day. Her life will improve because she will be showing others that tragedy did not wash her will to live out with the tide, and that in spite of the devastation, we can all continue to live and learn. The world will be a better place for having learned from her and people like her.

Dear George:

I have wanted to come for a session ever since my best friend died in 2009. But I have a question that I need to ask before I think about coming. Is it possible to block some souls from talking during a session? I know this sounds very strange, but I grew up in a very dysfunctional family—both parents were alcoholics, and have both since passed on. George, I know it sounds cruel, but I don't want to hear from them. They made my young years filled with pain, embarrassment, and humiliation—they would get drunk and pass out at my birthday parties. I could never have a friend stay over for fear they would see too much. And the last straw was when my mother came drunk to my college graduation. I can't seem to forgive them for the pain they caused, and I don't really care what they have to say now. I'm a grown woman with my own issues now, and I don't need to rehash the past. Is there any way you can block them from wanting to talk in a session? I would appreciate an answer.

—Susan

I wish my ability worked the way some people want it to. I also wish my ability worked the way *I* want it to. But at the end of the day, the session works the way the souls need and expect it to go—their way. The souls are in charge of the session nearly start to finish, and they communicate the things *they* have come to tell us. As much as I wish I could make the souls tell us what we want to hear, the souls know it is far more important and valuable to tell us what they know we *need* to hear. Sometimes we may not even realize how desperately we need to hear what the souls have come to tell us, until after they are done, and we can understand from their point of view why they do things the way they do.

Because of this, I've learned a long time ago that the souls have already looked into our hearts, understand the issues, and will speak to those issues we need to have addressed the very best they can. Whether or not we listen, heed their words, or walk away is of no consequence to the souls—they can and will tell us what they know we need to hear.

I cannot block any soul from communicating, nor would I ever want to. This also includes people the sitter may not want to hear from. There have been times in sessions when I know a soul who comes forward is not someone the sitter either intended to hear from, or even wanted to hear from. Although the souls already know why their loved ones are coming to the session, and what issues they know need to be addressed, there will still be that occasional wild card of a soul who wants to communicate in spite of their loved ones not wanting to hear from them. They do this because they seem to know better than we do what will really help during a session, and part of the reason souls even communicate from the world hereafter is to help us patch up and fill in the holes in our road to acceptance on the earth. Sometimes, those holes are the holes in our past that we don't want to look at, and we don't want to remember. But the souls know that part of understanding, repairing, and growing on the earth means having to face issues that we may have never before been able to face.

I can say with confidence that if Susan were to come to a session, her parents would most certainly feel the need to reach out to her. It would certainly be for reasons she may understand, but there will also be reasons she may not completely understand right now. But the souls know they have *this* opportunity to reach out to her, and for their benefit and hers, they will communicate. Even though I know it's not possible, if I actually did have the ability to filter the souls' communication, I would be hard-pressed to do it, even if a client requested it. The reason is very simple—we need to hear what they have to say. Very often, we are stuck with the last images of a life on the earth of our loved ones—sometimes good, but sometimes bad, and those are the images we replay over and over in our heads. We forget that life has gone on—we have changed, and in a very dramatic way the souls also have changed. They have already had the opportunity to see their lives on the earth in 360 degrees, and it brings them a new understanding of not only how their lives impacted them, but how their actions impacted others. I'm sure that once Susan's parents were able to see *from her point of view* the damage and pain they caused, it was a moment of shock, humiliation, and sadness for them. Part of each of the souls' continuing spiritual journey in the world hereafter is to fix what they may have broken on the earth, and to afford those to whom they were unkind, unthinking or irresponsible the benefit of their newfound love and peace. These souls take the responsibility of righting who and what they have wronged very seriously, and part of bringing that pain full circle to peace involves communicating to the loved ones they have hurt, if only to explain and apologize for what they have done. They do this for themselves, to continue learning and growing in the hereafter, but more important, they do it for *us*—to put the past firmly in the past so that we can also recover, learn from it, and move on.

There is never a point in our lives, either here or hereafter, when it is too late to say *I'm sorry*. There is also never a point in our journey when it is too late to hear how sorry those who hurt us truly are. It seems pretty clear to me that part of Susan finding her way back from the pain of her childhood is to hear the words her parents need to tell her, and to understand how important forgiveness is to her soul growth here. She cannot be a complete person and have a complete learning experience on the earth without it. I won't lie and say it's easy—it isn't. Often, in sessions like these where parents have to apologize to their children for unspeakable acts it brings the pain gushing back to the surface all over again. It brings anger, hurt, and tears, but all of it is necessary. At the risk of sounding like I am defending her parents, I have to say Susan may also be surprised at the degree of difficulty her parents also found in their own lives here—a life mired in alcoholism and loss of control is not a life anyone aspires to live. But things happen in life, we make bad choices, we do bad things, we learn from them when our lives move on to a more peaceful and constructive world, and we take this knowledge and try to pass it along to those who are still struggling with the effects of damage and pain in their own lives. It is only then that we can take what we have heard and either throw it away wholesale because we are not ready to forgive and move on, or we can admit that our inability to forgive is coloring everything in our lives, and we need to clear it up and continue with a glad heart.

The souls can communicate and apologize, they can tell

us they love us and they are helping to undo the damage they caused, but it is within each of our own life lessons to take responsibility also, and use what we have learned to try to fix what has been damaged within us. We have to find our way back from the hurt and pain so that we can walk forward again with some peace. Otherwise, we ourselves are doomed to make the same mistakes over and over. It is my hope that Susan will come to a session and allow her parents to tell her what she probably already knows somewhere in her heart but she really does need to hear. I hope she can listen without prejudice, and use the information to rebuild the hurt and pain into something more constructive and enduring. It is human nature to forgive, and also one of the hardest lessons we will learn while we are here. But once learned, forgiveness frees us and allows our soul to lighten just enough to continue moving through our journey here with a better understanding of those who failed us, and a much more complete picture of ourselves.

Dear George:

It's been twenty-seven months since I lost my darling son, Drew. I am finding life so hard without him. Each day brings more heartache than I can cope with. I feel so lost—I cannot cope with the fact that I did not save my boy. I did everything I could have, but cancer is a bitch

and she took him from me. Drew is an amazing person.
Why do they take them away from us? I am so broken-
hearted that life doesn't seem worth it anymore.

—*Karin*

I know how difficult it is to lose a child, and to feel helpless and unable to fix things and make it better when you see a child slipping away through illness. There is something terrible about having to face something like cancer stealing your child a piece at a time, and all you can do is watch and suffer. It would cause the best and most faithful of us to reel at the notion that there is any sense or justice in the world. The world goes mad for parents who have to witness the suffering of a child, and the wake of that storm has the power to take each of us away with it, if we let it. Karin's hope has been smashed, and rightly so. But perhaps understanding the rest of the story—the part we cannot see—might help her find some sense of hope that all is not lost. In fact, her boy and her hope now reside in a place not as far away as she may think. She will see her boy again when her own journey is over, and her hope is something that, if she works very hard to understand, can find its way back to her. It will help her continue to try to make sense of all this tragedy, and help her to continue her own journey until she sees Drew again.

You *did* save your boy, Karin. You saved him from illness, misery, and pain by loving him enough to let him go to his joy. We cannot see it, and sometimes we can't understand it, because all we can see is to the end of our physical plane. We do not know what else the souls and the world hereafter have in store for us—we can only rely on what we can believe in our own hearts to be true. But things are much, much better than we could even hope.

Cancer and other terminal illnesses have no power—they are just vehicles that take us from this world to the next when our time on the earth is done. Most of the souls don't even acknowledge their passing in this manner because even though they may have suffered, they have gained so much from it in terms of their new life of peace and joy that the temporary hardship of passing on through terminal illness hardly seems noteworthy after they have been dazzled by the hereafter. Though many souls will acknowledge having a rough time prior to their passing, and even recall having to suffer for a time, all of that seems so far in the distant past because the souls see how valuable it was to the new world they have built for themselves with their hard circumstances on the earth. They *survived* their suffering, and they live to tell us about how that last bit of learning on the earth blossomed into a world of joy for them.

It's very hard for us to understand the souls' point of view, and their complete understanding of why they had to suffer before passing, because we can't feel their joy, or know their peace, or understand how important this journey was to them *and* to us. What we see was just the end, but what the souls see is just the beginning. They are not mired in a sense of failure like we are, because they simply did not fail—they succeeded. They succeeded beyond their wildest dreams of succeeding. They've found a world of joy after their suffering, and they return to help us understand that if we could only see the picture in its entirety, we would also have no cause to suffer the passing of a loved one.

We, each of us, have to set out hearts straight and believe with every ounce of power we have that the Infinite Light knows exactly what it is doing, and there is a reason for everything we experience on the earth. The reward, as the souls have told me for more than forty years, is worth every second of the pain. That's a big statement for the souls to make, but we have to believe them because they were once in our shoes and they know how hard it is. We are still on the earth for a reason, and we need to find a way to continue, not just for our sake, but for the sake of those on the earth who still need us. Drew is in a world of peace and beauty so wonderful it's hard for any of us to truly imagine, but it does exist, and as soon as we are finished with our lifetime of struggle here, we will reunite with those we lost, and it will be as if grief never happened. That is something we can count on. Do you know what else we can count on? We can count on the fact that Drew walks every step of his mother's bereavement with her until she is able to walk it herself. That's a promise the souls make to each of us, and as long as we have a loved one in the hereafter, we are never alone on the earth.

Now is the point in Karin's life when she needs to find a way back to her hope. It is not easy, but it is vitally important to her journey here. I don't believe any of us can truly live on the earth in any kind of fashion if we do not have our hope to occasionally fall back on when our grief threatens to overwhelm us. So, Karin, fall down, have your cry, lash out—but at some point, you'll have to continue, not just for yourself but for everyone around you, including Drew.

There is something in Karin's letter that leads me to believe that she is on her way to feeling hope again. She wrote, *Drew is an amazing person.* She put that statement in the present tense, not in the past. That is clear proof that her heart does believe he continues. Her hope is not gone—just temporarily covered by pain. If she gives it time, Drew, himself, will tell her how proud he is that she found the will to continue. I promise you, from what the souls have told me, and from the small glimpses into their world I have been so fortunate to have seen, that if we can make it to the finish line, every second of it will have been worth it when we see all our loved ones again in a world of joy. If for no other reason, live for that fine day.

Dear George:

You have helped so many people all over the world, and you have brought such peace to people, even some couples I personally know who were very fortunate to have a session with you and hear your inspiring words from the souls.

My question may be a little unusual for you, but I thought it is just as important as the questions you answer for people who are in pain. I sometimes have my doubts about my beliefs, and they scare me sometimes. What about you, George? Have you ever found a time when your faith was rattled or your hope disappeared, even temporarily? I would love to know how you found your way back from that, because you are also human and experience the pain of so many people. I often think that your job must be the toughest job in the world, and there must be times when you throw your towel in and say "enough." I would bet your insight into your own fall of hope would be fascinating, and especially how you got it back.

—Jack

You know the old adage that "even cowboys get the blues"? Well, even mediums get the blues. Well, not so much the blues, per se—but those who work in the spiritual field sometimes experience a point where they doubt their own faith, and need to look past themselves for the inspiration and hope only the souls can provide. So, in essence, a little while ago, even this "cowboy" got the blues.

I know from my work with the souls that so many people, even the extraordinary souls like the saints, have had to grapple with their own occasional doubts about their own faith. After my own bout of spiritual doubt, I could easily understand how anyone could one day wake up and suddenly think that their hope and faith was maybe an illusion. I have heard this very sentiment from many, many people who have experienced a loss, even though they believe with all their heart that their loved ones live on. But hope and faith are funny things—they cannot be felt, or measured or weighed, except in your mind and heart. Inevitably, there will come that time when each of us, no matter how spiritual, will say, "but what if my heart and mind are wrong?"

My moment of doubt came recently, and very unexpectedly. For some reason, as my mind wandered during some mundane task on my day off, I thought about my mother. My mother was one of the rare few people in those early days of my career that was so convinced I was communicating with the souls that she was literally my number one fan. I say literally, because when I was working on the first-ever cable television show about psychic and mediumistic ability, *Psychic Channels,* my mother was so proud of her "Psychic George," as I was known then, that she wore a shirt around town that read: PSYCHIC GEORGE'S MOM. I thought at the time that she was crazy, but she was so proud and so unwavering in her belief in my ability that I conceded it was more sweet than crazy.

During my thoughts, it hit me that my mother had never really made communication to me in any solid, extended way since she had passed on. Yes, I had seen her in my mind on occasion, and heard from her very briefly, but it suddenly surprised me that the one person who was so sure of my ability never really took advantage of it to communicate at length about her life on the other side. Suddenly I wondered to myself why that could be, and I started feeling doubt about how and why *any* soul would want to communicate. I suddenly felt the fear that millions of people of faith feel at one time in their life or another—suppose it's just an illusion? Maybe we create it because we want so badly to hear it?

With everything I have heard and everything that I know about the souls in the last fifty years of hearing from them, you'd think doubt like this could never happen. But I am human, too, and my fears about faith and hope are the same as every other person out there. But I do know better. And because of that, I decided not to allow this kind of doubt into my mind. Instead, I decided to put the souls to the test.

I thought to myself, "If my mother is listening, then she will show me proof." I chose a symbol that would be pretty odd if I did see it—red feathers. It's not something you would come across every day, so the sight of it would definitely be something unusual for me.

Later that afternoon, a beautiful cardinal landed in the backyard and opened its wings as it landed very near me. "Too easy," I thought to the souls—"I see cardinals all the time. You have to do better."

Several days later, and having forgotten all about my fears and my demands of the hereafter to *prove* to me they are listening, I decided to go into New York City with my friends. Every Saturday on the West Side of Manhattan, there is an antiques flea market with the most unusual things you could find—everything from handmade items from many different cultures to furniture and clothing. I'm not much of a shopper, but we walked through the stalls of people selling their wares, and I found my own thoughts just wandering again—not looking at anything in particular—just enjoying the sights, the sounds, and the colors of the market. And there it was. It nearly hit me in the face.

I turned around because I thought I heard my name being called, and I nearly walked into a hat rack at one of the antiques stalls. I caught myself before I hit it, and as my eyes came back into focus, I was staring straight at an old-fashioned woman's hat among a few that were hanging on the stand. This one was inches from my nose. A hat made up completely of red feathers. At first I found it funny, but then my mind turned to gratitude to the souls who try so hard to save us from ourselves and our doubt. It was probably the ugliest hat I had ever seen, but it was covered in red feathers. I got the message. I also thanked my mom for working so hard to get it through my thick skull that she, like every one of the souls, has always been listening, no matter how crazy our thoughts about them may be, and no matter how persistent our doubt.

Of course the souls exist, and we know it very well. How could we not know? They help us every day, in ways we know and ways we could never imagine. Yes, have your doubt, think about it, wallow in it. Don't worry though—the souls are very patient. They will wait for you to remember they exist, and then they will continue to walk with you through every step of the way back to them.

Dear George:

Do people ever come to you just to find help for problems they are having? I don't have a lot of people who are passed on that I know, except for my grandma. But I have a problem that I was hoping maybe the souls could help me with.

I was in a marriage for four years to a man I thought was just wonderful, and for the first two years things were like Heaven. But after a series of financial setbacks, his beloved father dying and having to go through bankruptcy, everything about him changed. He got increasingly hateful and would say terrible things, and then he started hitting me. Even though I loved him so much I had to leave him for fear of my life. We divorced and I didn't see him again.

Now, three years later, we saw each other again at a mutual friend's home. He wants to try again, and has told me how sorry he is that he hurt me (he had written the same thing in letters to me as part of the therapy he went through). He seems different—maybe the therapy helped and maybe he just grew up a little. He wants to get back together, but I am so afraid, and my trust in him is gone. Can you ever go back and learn to trust somebody again? Have any of the souls you encounter talked about taking a chance again? I don't know if I'm being a fool, but I love him, and he was once such a good man. I

want to take a chance but I'm so scared and don't know
if my heart will ever fully love and trust him again.

—Laura

Many times, when the souls communicate, the lesson is not just for the loved ones the souls want to communicate to, but for me as well—I am always learning from the souls, and trying to grow in maturity of thought and spirituality, just like the people who come to see me. There seems to be so much to learn, and just when I think I have learned all I can, the souls expose another facet of humanity that surprises and sometimes even astounds me.

One of those facets is the issue of trust in our journey here—how fragile it can be, but how strong it can also be to withstand the trouncing each of us will receive in the course of a lifetime on the earth. We will undoubtedly encounter people who fail us or fail themselves, and we become the beneficiaries of misplaced or even broken trust. It is something each of us will experience, and how we rebuild the trust will say as much about our life lesson here as any other choice we will make for ourselves. Trust is not something we give ourselves, trust is a gift we give *each other*. It's a piece of ourselves that we entrust to those we feel worthy, and along with love, is probably the most important thing we will give another human being in our entire journey here.

Trust often takes a lifetime to build, but usually about a second and a half to destroy. So what happens when we place our trust in someone, only to have that person fail us? According to the souls, the answer is easy: We have to learn to trust again. Believe me, it isn't an easy statement for the souls to make, since many of them found themselves in the same circumstance as you. But the souls who have communicated about these same circumstances come back to me and their loved ones here with the same answer—to trust again is to be able to learn from the past, but to place hope in the future. The interesting wording of their answer holds the clue to why it is so important. We have to learn to trust others in order to grow, but we need to continue to learn from the past in order to succeed. To forgive and move on is wonderful, but to replace our trust in someone who has already failed us takes a bit of courage on our own part. We have to remember the past and not run away from it, or pretend it didn't happen. It *did* happen. But we have to look toward the future, understanding what we know, and make a judgment of trustworthiness based on someone else's sincere and honest request to *want* to be trusted again.

It's impossible for any one of us to know whether the decision to trust someone again is the right or wrong decision. Even though the souls may know, they are frequently not able to tell us, because they understand that our decisions will shape the rest of our existence here. That being said, it seems that the *decision* to trust is actually more important than whether we have placed our trust in the right people or not. That in itself is an entirely different lesson. When we begin to trust again, we return from that place of fear and uncertainty, and back into control of our own lives. *We* make the decision to trust—it is ours alone, and it is for our own soul growth. Whether the decision to trust pans out for us is perhaps part of another's life journey here. But finding and maintaining trust—earned or not—is part of what we must go through to become the fully rounded souls we must be to continue moving through this world and on to the next, where indecision, insecurity about our choices, and fear does not exist.

I'm not sure if the medium in me is reading too much into Laura's letter, but it does appear to me that her mind was made up even before she set pen to paper. And perhaps that's as it should be. It appears to me that although she has gone through a lot of pain, her heart finds some sense in learning to again trust somebody who she seems to love very much. It is scary to revisit the road that brought you pain and fear, but I and the souls believe it is much more scary to live in a world where we cannot trust those around us, or even ourselves, to come to the correct decision. Perhaps now, with history in the rearview mirror, and remorse in her former husband's heart, Laura can rebuild the trust she once had, and live up to her potential as a soul struggling on the earth to learn.

It is important to forgive, but not forget. Our memory of the past and what we have lived through is perhaps one of the best teachers we will have on our journey here. But our memory of the past is only a marker. We have to learn to remember the past without reliving it, and without holding it as ammunition further down the road. The souls have told us that whatever decision we do make on our own behalf or on behalf of somebody else, we must own it and own its outcome, and move on from it with a glad heart. Our lives here are about taking calculated chances—chances created by our memory of the past, plus the hope of a better future. Take the chance that matters to you the most, and look forward in hope.

Dear George:

Do we ever actually come back from loss?

—Glenn

This e-mail is perhaps one of the shortest I have ever received, yet the wording of that simple statement implies far more than you may even realize. I am assuming Glenn is speaking about the loss of a loved one, but that's not always the best assumption for me to make, because people also mourn the loss of a job, loss of a certain status in life, and sometimes, loss of themselves. I suppose it makes no difference the kind of loss, because the answer is usually the same for any aspect of loss. Yes, we do come back from whatever loss we have experienced, but in order to fully understand this answer we have to look beyond the confines of the world we know. The souls have told us that *all* loss comes full circle, and everything that has either eluded us on the earth, or was taken from us, will be found again in the world hereafter, where it is waiting for us.

So many of the souls who have communicated over the years, who themselves have suffered tragic losses of all different types, seem so matter-of-fact when they communicate about it from their world hereafter. The simple reason is that they have found once again whatever it was that they lost. But the more complex answer is that they understand why they had to experience that loss in the first place, and how in having lost, so many of them had found not only what they lost in the first place, but something far more precious— their own soul, and their ability to fully appreciate the often hard lessons of the earth.

We are so much like children on the earth—our lack of ability to understand what we can't know yet creates such pain and misery for us. We rail and thrash against whatever we think is keeping us from those we love and lost, circumstances that have come and gone, and opportunities that presented themselves and then disappeared. We fight, we cry, we curse, but we don't *think*. We don't think about what things actually mean against the backdrop of a lifetime of learning, and perhaps we really don't want to know. But in instances when we suffer loss of any kind, we have to think about why the outcome presented itself the way it did, and what we are actually supposed to learn from it.

I am sometimes a little surprised when families come to see me after the terminal illness of a loved one. They are heartbroken, and justifiably so. But I will ask them a simple question: "Would you rather have your loved one here, in pain and unhappy, or in the hereafter, young, happy, pain-free, and in peace and joy?" Many people need a minute to think about it before they seemingly begrudgingly say, "Well, in the hereafter, I guess." You would think we would trust our own faith, our hope, and everything we know, and be able to answer that question without a second's worth of hesitation. But many of us can't, because we don't quite understand that sometimes we have to give up the most precious things we have, though temporarily, to achieve peace. We simply aren't looking far enough up the road to know that everything scattered by the winds of our struggles on this earth, in this lifetime, comes back to us. And it all comes back to us because we have earned it with a lifetime of learning, growing, and understanding, just like those who we love have done before us. So the problem is really about understanding. We simply don't understand the concept of loss, and how it relates to our life on the earth. This is where the souls can be at their most valuable to us, because they have seen the world they thought they lost their most precious possessions to, only to find them again, experienced the peace and joy of having found them, and then wondered at the end of the day what all the fuss was about.

I know I have told this story to many families in sessions, and also in a previous book, but the message is so profound that it bears repeating often. I had a visitation in my sleep once with St. Anthony, the Catholic patron saint of things lost. Although I have experienced many visitations with the saints so they could help me understand more about my work and what the souls are hoping I can tell the rest of the world about their existence, this visitation went to the very heart of what we fear most in loss, and why we need to believe in the souls and what they are trying to tell us. In the visitation, St. Anthony took me to a beautiful lake in an area of woodlands that shone like emeralds in the sun, and even the grass seemed energetic and alive. We sat down next to the crystalline water, and he showed me a golden ring in his outstretched palm. "See," he told me, "if I took this ring, and threw it into the lake, it would be gone forever. But if I took this ring and held it in the palm of my hand, it would still be lost to you, but you would always know where it was. Hope makes it possible to believe that one day it will return to you. This is the very essence of our loss."

So there we have it—if we believe, then nothing is truly ever gone from us, it is only in a place just out of our reach for the time being. If we don't believe, then all we are left with is our cold, dark thoughts of loss. But something happens to each of us when we experience loss, and whether we acknowledge it or not, it is always there. Perhaps it is a gift from the souls in order to bolster our faith and help us believe, but after a loss, we are forever connected to the world hereafter by a chain of love that may be imperceptible to us, but we can feel it tugging every once in a while. I rather like to think of it as when we used to build tin can telephones as kids—two cans with a string attached between them. Yes, the connection is poor and we may not be able to hear a thing, but the tension on the string is still there, and we know there is somebody holding the other end. When we think about our own loss, if we concentrate hard enough, we can experience the faint tension on the string that keeps us connected to everything we have lost, because we know it is still connected. We have to be able to bring that same simple faith to our own loss, and know for sure that something is keeping the tension on that string for as long as we are able to keep it close to us.

The souls understand that loss—any loss—is painful. But once we finish our existence here, and earn the world we have been struggling for so long to find, everything we lost is found again, and the pain is gone forever.

One funny aspect of the souls when they communicate is their apparent amnesia when it comes to concepts like pain, worry, and fear, especially the souls who have been there for a while. They remember the circumstance, but they forget the *feeling* of what it was like, and I could think of no better reward for those who struggled here so much—to forget what it was like to ever have struggled. Yes, the souls understand what we are going through, and they sympathize, but they also know that in a matter of time, our pain will be a distant memory and that none of it matters anymore, in a world of peace. No more struggle—what a beautiful thing to look forward to. The souls make it very clear that this is their reward for having lived on the earth, gone through the pain, the suffering, the problems and the shortcomings, only to come out the other end in a world of understanding and joy. We can bear out the time we have on the earth, and even accept the things we know we must live through, if we can only hang on to that hope that it is there waiting for us when our time here is done. The only thing the souls and I can tell people who fall in their hope, or allow doubt to creep into their beliefs, is to hold on to that string—because those who hold the other end will never, never let go.

CHAPTER SEVEN

Touched by the Souls

Dear George:

Does everyone have the ability to talk to the souls?

—Virginia

I've always found that the easiest questions are often the hardest to explain. I think it's because the answer is often so simple that people don't actually believe it. But the answer to this question is *yes*, and the way to talk to the souls is to just open your mouth and talk. This is where the laughter usually comes in when I answer this question in a group—for some reason, people don't believe it's that easy. I go on to explain that you don't even have to open your mouth if you don't want to. You just open up your heart and let your thoughts out. The souls will hear you.

Now, I have a question. Why is this so hard to believe?

The souls have told me over forty years of sessions that they hear every single word we tell them, even if those words are trapped in our hearts and we can't quite get them out. The souls know exactly what is on our minds and in our hearts, especially with regard to our feelings for them. They hear everything we tell them, and they also hear everything we *want* to tell them, but somehow can't or won't. The souls have the ability to look right into us and understand our love, our pain, our restlessness, and our fear, especially when our thoughts involve them or their welfare. No matter how alone we think we are with our thoughts, the souls know that as long as we have a loved one in the hereafter, we are never alone in our thoughts, or in our own hearts.

One of the things that invokes surprise, and sometimes a little bit of fear in people who come to see me, is that I do not allow them to ask me questions of their loved ones during the session. There is a very simple reason for it. I know that the souls don't disappear from our lives simply because they have passed on to the world hereafter—they are still with us, still listening, and still trying to help us cope after loss. Part of their spiritual journey in the hereafter is to continue helping us through ours here, so there is no point in our lives where the souls are not part of the goings-on and intricacies of our lives. So there is basically no reason for us to even have to ask the questions we need answers to in a session—the souls know, and they will accommodate those questions and issues without our even having to ask. This is part of their wanting to show us just how connected to us they still are, and hearing it directly from the souls, without prompting through questions, helps many people understand just how much the souls are with us in our lives and in our struggles.

Whatever we think, whatever we feel, and whatever issues we face in our lives seems to register right onto the consciousness of the souls. They are always there when we need them, and they are listening to us and trying to help us to find ways to deal with the continuing journey on the earth. It really shouldn't be too hard to believe at all. If we put ourselves in the souls' shoes, what would we do? Of course we would hover over those we love and care about them constantly—it would go without question. It should not be hard to believe that the souls can hear us, they can see us, and they will do whatever they can to help.

Now I will play the medium and answer the next question Virginia has: Can the souls talk to us? The answer, again, is yes. The souls have never *stopped* talking to us, but we often can't hear them the way we can hear those on the earth who talk to us. The souls live in a different dimension than we do, and because their world is not bound to the concepts of physicality like ours is, we have to think differently about how the souls can touch and speak to us from a world not bound by the limitations of this one. The souls mostly talk to us telepathically. They don't always need words, but they can speak volumes into our minds and into our hearts, which can pick up this kind of transmission from them. But because we are only used to our ears hearing communication, we often have trouble discerning the difference between what is real and what we think our own minds have manufactured. We can't manufacture a sense of well-being or the overwhelming peace the souls can bring when they communicate to us in a way our heart or head will understand. It is often actual communication that people discount wholesale, simply because they can't trust their own ability to accept that the souls are actually *speaking*. Once we get past the hurdle of our own disbelief, we can allow the souls to speak to us in ways that may actually surprise us—through dreams when we sleep, through subtle signs during our day, and by filling our hearts with peace.

Dear George:

Do you know if souls choose us as parents before birth? I was wondering about this as I had a dream during pregnancy that my daughter was holding her arms out to me saying "Kiyoko!" over and over again. I wrote it down and looked it up and the meaning in Japanese is "Holy child." She is not of Japanese descent, but I was reading a book the night before by a Japanese man and am aware that logically it could have been a trigger for the dream . . .

but what are the chances I would make up that name
and a very old name at that?

—*Rebecca*

The souls have told me many times over the years that before a soul makes the decision to return to the earth, if it ever does, it will find the perfect circumstance in which to be born, in order to fulfill its spiritual journey and learn the lessons it came back to the earth in order to learn. The souls get to choose the time, the place, and the people they will share their journeys with, in order to find the opportunities they need with which to fulfill their purpose here. A secondary part of this plan is for the soul to be a part of somebody else's journey on the earth, because each of us will be a player in another's life lesson. There needs to be the circumstance of a soul wanting to return to the earth, into the circumstance they can learn and grow in, and to be a part of the ongoing journey of a family already on the earth. When all the pieces come together, another baby is born to the earth.

I realize that by explaining the actual process in its most simple terms, it all seems rather clinical or devoid of any emotion. That's not the case at all, especially with regard to the souls who choose to come back to the earth. The souls, before they do anything regarding their decision to return to the earth, get to know us in a way that helps them decide if the choice to come to the earth is the right one for them.

They learn about us, and they come to love us for the people we are. They come to love our circumstance on the earth, and they understand the journey we are on as well. They want to be a part of our lives and journeys on the earth, and the decision to go ahead and be the child we hoped for is made with great anticipation from the souls.

One of the most poignant examples of this kind of love from the souls came in a session where a couple had lost a baby they named Elisabeth. I often have to explain to people that although their child may have been an infant on the earth, without the ability to speak, when they are unencumbered by a physical body, their soul can speak quite well, and is not of any determined age. It sometimes makes it a little difficult to pin down an age of a child, because they may seem much wiser than their time on the earth. But during the session, Elisabeth held up her hand and showed me five fingers. My immediate reaction was to think she was five years old, but I had to wait and really listen—she was trying to tell me that she was on the earth only five days.

It's heartbreaking sometimes to watch a couple fall apart after the loss of a child they had waited for, dreamed about, and already had such high hopes and plans for, only to have something go terribly wrong and find themselves bereaved parents when they should be celebrating the birth of a beautiful child. Elisabeth showed me that she had a rather rare congenital heart problem, and despite the hospital's best efforts, she could not survive here. It is often very hard for people to understand that sometimes a learning lesson for the souls will only be five days, but the learning lesson of having a child pass on in our lifetime is for our own spiritual growth. It makes no difference to the souls how long their stay will be here—even if it is for only hours or days. They have fulfilled what they came here for, and they try to help us understand that a child is a child, whether it is on the earth or in the hereafter. We love the child just the same, and for the rest of our lives.

In this session, however, Elisabeth said an extraordinary thing: "I chose you to be my parents because you both had a heart full of love." And then, to the woman, she said, "I loved you even before you were my mother, and I will always be your daughter." For me, this was a very powerful reminder that not everything that defines our journey here is as strict and rigidly planned as it sometimes seems from the souls. *Love* is still an important factor in their decision-making process. It's nice to know that even though the souls need a specific circumstance to be born into, they *love* us and want to be part of our lives. Perhaps that's the best thing to know about a child—they choose you because they love you.

Regarding the second part of this question, no one can really know how much of our dream is placed there by the souls, or added by our subconscious. What we do know is that there is definitely a combination of *both*. I immediately recognized the name Kiyoko because I worked in Japan a few times, and the word comes up frequently when children communicate from the hereafter to help their parents understand that they are being well taken care of and they are living in a world of love and joy. I wish I could tell you how much of the dream was inspired by the souls, but perhaps only you can answer that. But the souls often speak to us in our subconscious, if only to help prepare us and bring us to a place of understanding. Sometimes it's obvious where our subconscious thoughts have kicked in during this kind of dream. Often, when we have unhappy or fearful thoughts, those are *never* a product of the souls' communication, but a manifestation of our own fear projected onto the dream. If it brings us peace and hope, then it's a good bet it came from the souls, who only bring peace and happiness with them when they communicate. So we should split the difference in our head, and give some credit to the souls, and some credit to ourselves. I'm wondering if Rebecca did actually name her daughter Kiyoko. Perhaps one day she can tell me herself.

Dear George:

My sister was scheduled to see you in session in October 2006, but the appointment had to be rescheduled for eight weeks later because you had to go in for heart bypass surgery. She had a wonderful session and I thank you for that, but my question is about you, actually. Since I know that they must temporarily stop the heart during bypass surgery, did you experience a Near Death

*Experience, or anything unusual, given the ability you
have to hear from the souls? I hope I'm not dredging up a
bad time for you, but I know a lot of people are so interested in what you hear and see, and I would think that
during something unusual like surgery, the souls may
have something important to tell you. Did they?*

—Ronald

In October 2006, I apparently won the lottery of genetics,
and doctors found several blockages in my arteries.
Although it was quintuple bypass surgery, it all happened so
fast. I was scheduled for surgery within a week, had the surgery, and was out of the hospital four days later. Getting
back to a normal routine did take a few weeks, but I can honestly say that I have never felt better in my life, and because
of my Irish/English genetic proclivity toward high choles-
terol and a family tree full of heart problems, I took care of
something that had the potential to be fatal if let go too long.
But all in all, it was a good experience, almost no pain at all
at any point before or after, and a bit of a learning lesson as
well.

I find it funny that your exact question was the question
du jour when I was fully awake the day after surgery. My
coauthor, Andrew, who had spent the entire day and most of
the night until he was browbeaten by the hospital staff into
leaving, came in early the next day with only two questions:
"How are you feeling?" and "Who came by when you

were under?" The first question was rather plain to see, because I was already sitting up and feeling very good, but the second question I had to think about a little bit. There seemed to be one point when I knew I was under anesthesia that I heard what seemed like hundreds of voices—just a mixture of people talking, and I would only be able to pick up a word here and there in the jumble. The conversation seemed to be about me, and not necessarily *to* me, but I could tell there were a lot of souls communicating. It's not unusual to hear that, because that is sometimes what I hear in sessions—a lot of people talking at once, until a particular soul or souls comes forward and the rest retreat in order to let the souls who need to speak have the opportunity. This seemed slightly different though, because I felt I was with them, almost like being in a crowded room with your eyes closed, and only being able to hear instead of see.

But at another point in the five-hour surgery, I distinctly felt and "saw" two very familiar and comforting figures— souls who seem to be following me my entire life on the earth. The first was a soul I affectionately call the "Lilac Lady"—a name I gave this soul when I first saw her when I was six years old. She is so named because she comes surrounded by a tremendous amount of light that has a lilac-colored hue, and always comes around me with kindness and understanding many times in my life. I have come to understand later in my life that the "Lilac Lady" is actually St. Jeanne d'Arc, or Joan of Arc, who herself was a seer when she lived on the earth in the 1400s. She is credited with using her ability to lead the French army to victory during the Hundred Years' War, but was captured and burned at the stake when she was nineteen years old. She has always represented strength and grace to me, and has seen me through many difficult times, both in my young life, and later on in my career as a medium. It did not surprise me in the least that she appeared at that time, if only to represent herself and allow me to know she was "in my corner."

Another figure that I "saw" distinctly was St. Catherine Labouré—another enduring and familiar figure, who not only has been around me for many years as a type of mentor, but someone more than a few people have actually witnessed around me. Interestingly enough, St. Catherine was also a visionary, and is credited with having seen a vision of the Blessed Mother, who showed her a symbol of herself in an oval frame, surrounded by stars, which later became the first Miraculous Medal of the Blessed Mother. What I have always found amazing about St. Catherine's interest in my life is the words told to her by the Blessed Mother, which ring so clearly in my own mind and heart—"God wishes to charge you with a mission. You will be contradicted, but do not fear—you will have the grace to do what is necessary." I was aware of St. Catherine's presence during the surgery, very much in the same manner as she has come to me when I am sleeping—sitting in what seems to be a small chair, and in great contemplation. It seems she "speaks" to me without words, preferring instead to speak directly to my mind and my heart without having to say anything aloud. Although I am never conscious of the things she has told me, I know my heart and mind have understood everything she has said. I believe that her intent is always to speak to my soul, and not necessarily *me*—as if there are things I must know, but I must not be conscious of, for fear that I would dismiss them or question too much.

It may be surprising to know that others who know me over the years have also seen—with varying degrees of fear and wonder—the vision of St. Catherine sitting to the right of me while I sleep. One of the first to see St. Catherine at my bedside was Andrew, my coauthor, during a tour stop in Kansas City for the book *Lessons from the Light*. I remember waking from my sleep with the feeling of being watched, only to find Andrew in the door frame of my bedroom, wide eyed. "There was somebody sitting right next to your bed!" he told me. Although Andrew is no stranger to the phenomena that happen around me with regard to the souls, this one surprised him because he could see her so clearly. She was bathed in a golden light, with the top of her tricornered cornette shining. Another time, a relative who was supposed to stay with her mother at my home for a few days made a rather hasty exit after the first night, claiming a need to return home. It wasn't until months later that I found out from her mother that she had also seen St. Catherine, who she described as a "lady with a triangular hat" as she passed my room that night on the way to the bathroom. It frightened her so much that she did not want to stay at the house—something I found sad, but completely understandable.

I always feel very fortunate and grateful that the Extraordinary Souls, like St. Catherine, St. Jeanne, St. Anthony, and many others, make regular appearances in my life, because it represents a sign of faith that they believe in me, believe in my work, and want to encourage me to continue to "have the grace to do what is necessary." It was especially nice to know they took the time to visit me during my surgery, and I always consider their appearances the same as old, dear friends who come by because they care. Were that each of us were able to recognize the times that the souls of our own loved ones were around us, helping us to continue on our road here, and being a positive force in each of our lives. It would probably initially scare the *bejesus* out of some people, but I think with time and understanding, we would find more benefit in their appearances than we would reasons to fear them. There is never anything to fear from the souls, who come with love and peace. It's up to us to take their visits for what they truly are—a sign of hope, and a true sign that they believe in us.

Dear George:

I know you are a great medium, but even Babe Ruth did not hit a home run every time he was at bat. Did you ever have a session that just didn't work, or nobody showed up from the other side?

—Gil

In more than forty years of sessions and a little more than thirty-five thousand sessions, I have never had an occasion where the souls have not come through. This is no great tribute to my ability, but rather a tribute to how much the souls want to communicate with us. Although the souls know that they can communicate to each and every one of us in ways they hope we will understand and grasp, they also know that my ability to "pick up" or discern their communication is something they rely on in order to speak in a clearer way to their loved ones. They want to be able to help us understand that they continue, that they are happy and at peace, and that they are still part of our ongoing lives.

While I can say with every confidence that the souls are always 100 percent accurate, I can also tell you most assuredly that I am *not*. The souls understand that there is a bit of a game at play when they use me to communicate. They have to help me to understand what they want to communicate, frame it in a way my own brain will understand, and hope I communicate what they are trying to get across to their loved ones. Although I've learned to listen as carefully as I can to the souls in session, there will always be something I don't understand, or information my own brain will fight because it does not make sense to me. The souls are often pretty patient with me, as they try to move past the thinking part of my brain to the unconscious part, in order to get their messages across without the conscious part of my brain trying to edit and overthink their words. This is the only sticking point in the session—the souls have to rely on me and my humanness, get me to remove my involvement in their thoughts, and get me to communicate what they came to tell their loved ones. Sometimes, it's very easy for the souls to do. But sometimes my brain may fight them, because my conscious mind cannot grasp the message they are trying to convey. This forces them to have to find another way to tell me the information they want me to pass along, in a way my brain can understand and accept. Eventually, however, and no matter how much my brain wants to fight a particular message, the souls always win and get their point across—one way or another.

I have been told that my accuracy hovers around 98 percent, which is pretty amazing, given how the souls have to step carefully through the minefield of my own thoughts, ideas, and biases—especially when it comes to them. I still make the souls prove they are communicating by sometimes pushing them for clarity, especially when they try to communicate information I myself do not understand. But at the end of the day, the souls do whatever they can to push past the conscious side of my brain, and communicate the messages they need to tell loved ones, without too much involvement on my part.

I think the analogy about Babe Ruth is a very good one. Although the souls are able to communicate with no problem at all, there are times when I sidetrack myself by concentrating too much on just one soul, and I forget to "look around" for others who also want to communicate, or I try to jump the gun by assuming I know where the souls are going with something, only to be told I am completely off the mark. The good news is that if things do go off the rails when I think too much during the session, the souls can quickly bring it back on track by telling me to stop, regroup mentally, and listen carefully as they speak.

No matter what goes on in the session, however, the success of the communication seems to sit squarely with the sitter's ability to understand and accept what the souls have come to tell them. Again, in the vast majority of sessions, people come hoping to hear whatever the souls have to say, but there will be some who have expectations and their own agenda. The meeting of the expectations on the part of the sitter, with the reality of what the souls know we need to hear, often determines if the sitter deems the session a success. Sometimes the souls can accommodate everything the sitter wants and needs to know. And sometimes, they can't. There are occasions when there is information the souls simply cannot tell us because it will interfere with the life journey we have yet to complete. There is some information a sitter will expect to hear that they cannot know, and the souls will not tell them. Although that is usually fairly rare, it does happen, and again, the sitter may understand, and find success in the communication—or not, and find no value in the souls' words.

I don't like the word *expectation*. The word implies that we have some control over a world we have absolutely no control over. Yet, amid all this chaos, we have the *expectation* that things will go a certain way. Sometimes the expectation is justified. If you throw the ball into the clown's mouth five times out of five tries, then there is a reasonable expectation you will make six. But I have found in my years of communication with the souls, that if you have the expectation to throw words into the souls' mouths, then expectation is bound to let you down.

I have been very lucky in my years as a medium that the majority of people who come to see me truly want only to hear from their loved ones, without any expectation of what the souls may or may not communicate. They only want to know that the souls actually *are* there, that they are happy and at peace, and that they continue to follow us on the earth.

But there will always be that one appointment where nothing the souls say will help, and people feel let down by the communication because it didn't address the issues *they* came to hear about. Worse than that, for a rare few, their feeling is that the session was a total failure. There is good and bad news after a session like that. The good news is that regardless of what they didn't hear in the session, the sitter's belief in their loved ones remains intact, but the bad news is that it's all my fault, or the fault of my ability. Frankly, I prefer that they blame me rather than their loved ones for the inability of the session to go their way. But it will never change the fact that in all the things the souls can tell us, there are things that they simply can't, no matter how much we expect they will. And no matter what I do or say, I have understood from the souls a long time ago that I cannot make the souls say what the sitter wants to hear.

I recently had a woman come to see me hoping to hear from her father. He came through talking about a mistake she made on the earth, and how she was going to have to let it go and accept the consequences. He had some real words of wisdom for her, and talked at length, trying to help her to help herself. It became obvious near the end of the session that this woman had no intention of taking this advice, and it was more obvious that she certainly did not want to hear it. Needless to say, the session, in her eyes, was a failure, and all her father (and myself for that matter) can do is hope that at some point in her life, the words will ring true in her heart. But it was obvious she did not want to hear advice from her father—she wanted facts, directions, and specifics as to how to direct her life. I suppose if she were coming for her own needs and to have her life figured out for her, then I agree—the session was a failure.

We cannot expect that the souls will say what we want to hear, do what we want them to do, and fix whatever is broken in our lives. What they do, instead, is give us the courage to face a new direction, or to help us understand a different way of thinking from their unique vantage point. But those who think the souls will cater to them—actually rather, *pander* to them, will find themselves very quickly and very thoroughly disappointed in the sessions. The souls will never take away from us the very reason why we are here—to walk the walk, live the life, put out the fires or accept the consequences when we won't or can't. This is our road, our life, our struggle, our accomplishment.

When you bought this book, you had no idea what I was

going to write here. You have a reasonable expectation that it will be something about life hereafter, and something helpful, but you can't expect me to address every issue in the universe, or make me write what you were hoping to read. You can't expect that because I am human, I have my own thought process, and my own ideas. I wonder what happens to people when they forget that their loved ones still have their own thought process, and that they are still human. The souls don't become mindless beings whose only job is to "fix" us. They understand better than we do that life here is our own journey. They can help as much as they can try, but the rest is up to us to live it and do it. The souls do the best they can in every circumstance to help us feel loved, cared about, and they try to offer their thoughts and ideas to us—not to change our direction, but rather, to *give* us a direction. So that we understand we are all walking toward something, regardless of the path.

I find the sessions that don't go well for the sitter are not any different from the ones that do. The souls talk, they help, they prod, they do whatever they can. I truly think the difference is our intent in coming to the session, and the manner in which we perceive and accept what the souls have come hoping to help us understand. Some sitters are selfish. They have no interest in the souls insofar as how much the souls can clue them into some part of their own lives. I know they believe their reasons for hearing from the souls are good and forthright, but at the end of the hour (and sometimes longer, since I see the unresponsive faces and dejected looks, and my own human nature tries to pry more information from the souls) the souls did not do enough for them, no matter how much they actually did say. I have often said that the souls will help us—they will give us the keys, the map, and the car, but they will not drive for us. That is entirely up to us. We cannot have the expectation that the souls, now that they have figured it all out for themselves, will figure it out for us as well. The souls know far too well that how we overcome our struggles is the true test on the earth; they cannot help us cheat. They can do and say so much during a session, but if we don't find it useful, if we don't take their perspective into account or understand why they can and cannot address some issues, then it has no value to us. I find that to be the saddest part of these "failures"— that because the sitters key issue is not examined, or ongoing problems resolved, then all the words of the souls have no value to them. So in that sense, it really is a failure, and a tremendous waste of the souls' time and energy.

In all fairness to the sitters who come, it will sometimes happen that the fault of missing communication is *mine*. I simply goof—I don't listen carefully enough, or I don't give the souls enough latitude to fully explain some of the points they are trying to make. One good thing that does happen in circumstances like these is that the souls will try to regroup and try it again with me—they will make me go back, sometimes to square one, and *make* me listen more carefully to what they want to communicate. Although the souls eventually win out over my apparent stubbornness, sometimes the bobble in the session leaves the sitter unsure about the session in its entirety, which I find very sad indeed. It is very clear that but for my own missteps or failure to listen completely to the souls, what the souls do have to say, and how they say it, is of great value and importance, no matter how many times they had to try to force it through my thick skull.

We heard from a woman recently who had posted a review on one of the books written about me, claiming her session was a failure because her husband came through to dominate the session, but near the end of the session, she had to prod me into looking around for another soul who she asked might be there. After stopping and going back I realized that there was, in fact, another soul waiting pretty patiently to communicate. It was the woman's son, who'd passed on shortly after the father. Although the son was able to communicate and did, somehow, having to prod me into looking for more souls made the woman feel that the session was a failure. She also went so far as to say the accuracy of the session was only due to the "fact" that her circumstance was researched by me. When I hear things like that, then I feel really badly for the sitter, because I know the souls' words didn't register. At all. They got stuck on the mechanics and not on the *words of the souls.*

It seems preposterous to think that hundreds of sessions can be researched. We even encourage people not to use their actual names or information when they make an appointment. In actuality, who they are is irrelevant to the session; it's the souls who communicate and usually the personal information they share could never be found in a public record. But people will sometimes "throw the baby out with the bathwater" because they are at the edge of their hope, and need things to go perfectly in order to believe. I wish that could be the case all the time, but that is simply not the world we live in. I think that one day, if the souls are able to figure out how to speak through a computer, they'd have nearly a 100 percent success rate with the sitters, because they have taken out their biggest obstacle in a session—having to filter their information through my human brain. But I also say *nearly* 100 percent, because I know from years of sessions that no matter how hard the souls work, there are simply people who cannot or will not accept what the souls have come to tell them. It is not as important though, because the souls' words are not only for now, but tomorrow, and well into our future. The souls know that if their loved ones don't understand or accept right away, they will, *eventually*. Over the years we have gotten a call or a letter from someone who was unhappy with a session, and called me every name in the book, only to write back sometimes a year later to apologize and tell us the session was everything they could hope for and more. So what changed? Not the session—it was over quite some time ago. What changes is our ability to understand, accept, and take to heart what the souls had tried so hard to make us understand in the first place. No matter when it happens, I'm just glad it does happen. The words and thoughts of the souls are just too important and valuable to our lives here to discount wholesale. But like everything else, no matter what people initially think of the session, there will be a point where the words will sink in and become clear and meaningful to each of us. It is only then when the souls, and even I for that matter, can truly consider the session a success.

Dear George:

My husband and best friend was killed in March 2009; we had just had our twenty-sixth anniversary that January. We have been best friends since I was eight and he was twelve. We were married when I was sixteen years old. He was murdered, and I miss him so much that sometimes the pain is so intense that I feel like I can't go on. I have been waiting and waiting for something from him—a sign, a dream, or to see him again. Something. I need to know he's okay and for him to know that I love him and miss him dearly.

—Kimberly

I certainly understand Kimberly's pain, but I need to tell her something that I tell every person who is asking for a sign from their loved ones, and it is pretty simple—*stop asking*. I know that may sound very cruel, but we need to consider what the souls are trying to do for us, even in spite of ourselves: They are trying to keep us to our path here, and not allow the pain and fear of having a loved one passed on to derail the rest of our journey on the earth. They know how important it is for each of us to keep moving, even when we are heavily burdened with grief, because it is the only way we will find our way out of the maze of this lifetime and back to those we truly love in the world hereafter.

There is one thing I can say that I hope will make everyone feel a little better—the souls know the day and the hour we will be able to receive a sign from them, and they look forward to that time almost as much as we do. They want to be able to show us that we are loved, that they are still around, and that they are still helping us in our grief. The only problem is that we sometimes are not moving well enough through the struggle of loss, and the souls know they cannot pull us backward into our grief by showing us signs and providing a constant reminder that they are not physically with us on the earth. The souls would never do anything like that—the continuation of our journey here is much too important to them. So they must wait until they know we are handling our grief well enough to receive evidence from them that they live, and that they are continuing their lives while also being part of ours.

I often ask people what they would do if they started receiving dreams on a daily basis from their loved ones, or if they started receiving signs on an hourly basis that they were not alone. Most have confessed that they wouldn't get out of bed, or they would just live from sign to sign. It's understandable, but it's not what the souls know we should be doing right now. So they don't complicate our lives by throwing in too many reasons not to face our losses and try to continue in spite of them. The souls know how important our journey on the earth is, and there is nothing they can or would do to take the very valuable lesson of moving past loss from us. To do that would be to change the course of our lifetime here permanently.

Kimberly loves and trusts her husband, so she should take comfort in the fact that no matter what, he would make the best decisions possible for the both of them. This is where the *rubber meets the road* with regard to our faith in the souls— we have to believe that they have our best interests at heart, and that they know when and where they will be able to show us they are still with us.

We need to give it time, and let the souls decide the best time and the best way to show us how much we are loved. I guarantee it will happen—the souls will never let us down.

Dear George:

I had a wonderful visitation from my mother in a dream just a few weeks ago. I dreamt that we walked through the park near my childhood home, and even though I am an adult now, she spoke to me as if I were a little girl again, telling me how much she loved me and how she is always going to help me when I need it. It was such a wonderful dream. But as the days went by, my cynicism caught up with me, and I'm not sure if it was actually a

*visitation or wishful thinking. How can you tell the dif-
ference, and will the souls really come to us in a dream to
make us feel better?*

—Alyssa

The souls can and do communicate to us in a sleep state,
mainly because they know that our unconscious minds
can more readily accept the notion of a visitation that our
conscious minds may reject entirely. Once the souls can get
past that part of us that causes our disbelief, they can speak
clearly to us, and help motivate us in our lives. Under the
guise of a "dream state," the souls can be as specific and
descriptive as they want, and the part of our brain that con-
trols our dreams will not only listen, but accept and hold the
information the souls want to tell us.

I have been the subject of many research and medical
tests over the years, in places like Cornell University Medical Center, The University of Las Vegas, The University of
Virginia, and the University of Arizona. In one of the tests,
my brain was subjected to thermographic imaging, to show
which part of the brain was at work while I was hearing from
the souls. In what surprised the researchers, the imaging
showed my brain to actually be "asleep"—even though I was
fully awake, while I was hearing communication with the
souls. They theorized that although I am fully awake during
the sessions, the soul speaks to that part of my brain in the
subconscious so that my conscious brain does not fight the

information coming in from the souls. It helps explain a lot about why the souls choose a sleep state in which to contact most of us—it is there where their words can do the most good.

Many people worry about whether a "dream" was an actual visitation or simply wishful thinking. There are distinct differences that most people realize, only after having a bona fide visitation from a loved one in a sleep state. While dreams stay nebulous and never seem to come close to specifics, the visitations take on the characteristics of actual life, and they *feel* different. Many people have reported touching objects, feeling themselves walk, reacting to the temperature of the air that surrounded them, and feeling some peculiarities that are associated specifically with the souls. Some of those peculiarities that seem to come up often when people talk about their visitations is the *cold*—people seem to sense cold whenever they move toward the souls. Others have said that they can feel the energy that emits from the souls, and even that energy feels palpable and real.

But what seems to be the defining factor in an actual visitation from the souls seems to be the immense feeling of love and joy—something so strong that it cannot be produced in a dream. People have reported both feeling joy and peace in their visitation. These kinds of feelings are too tall an order for a simple dream, and because of the strong sense of joy people feel both during, and sometimes weeks after the visitation, it takes on a kind of reality dreams can never do. We may dream of our loved ones, and have a lovely dream at that, but when we begin to feel, sense, and enjoy the energy from the souls, it helps us to understand the difference between a common dream and an actual visitation.

Many people write to me because they experience horrible dreams that they feel are actual visitations. In their dreams, their loved ones are upset or in some kind of peril, where they plead for our help. The experience usually leaves them badly shaken or worried. There is usually an easy explanation for why so many people associate their nightmares with visitations from the souls, and the reason why it happens may surprise you. Many of the nightmares are actually attempts by the souls to communicate to us, and just as they enter our subconscious, something within us tries to justify their presence, and pulls up our grief and fear, building a nightmare scenario around what we are seeing and feeling. So they must abandon the communication, but our brains don't abandon the nightmare—we see it through until it scares us awake or produces all kinds of terrible feelings.

Just like the dream, however, the nightmare is not real—things make no sense, we cannot feel the joy of the souls, and it is simply a projection of fear and grief that throws itself onto the canvas of what could have been actual communication from the souls. It's sometimes hit and miss for the souls when they try to comfort us and bring us a sense of peace when they know we are in a state that would be much easier than in waking life to listen, to accept, and to understand.

Visitations of loved ones bring with them such peace and comfort that the differences, when you do have an actual visitation, will seem very clear. I find it interesting that in her visitation Alyssa was younger than she is now, but it very well could have been her mind's way of listening without prejudice to the words her mother was telling her. The fact that she felt and saw herself walking in a very familiar place has the ring of a true visitation to it, as well as the clarity of the message from her mother. Also, the fact that it took her days for her brain to discount the adventure shows that the effects of it lingered more than just the few seconds an actual dream would have, so it may very well have been a bona fide visitation that she experienced.

When people do experience a visitation, I think they may look too hard into it for reasons or explanations. There is no need to dissect a wonderful experience—just live it, accept it, and thank whomever was kind enough to come by in order to help you cope and continue. The souls want to help us in any way they can—if we let them—and when they do, we need to see it as a kind and loving gesture, without trying too hard to find the root of it and analyze too much. Just do what I do when the souls come to visit me—say thank you, take the information to heart, and move on.

Dear George:

I am in the middle of reading Dianne Arcangel's book Afterlife Encounters. *Like everybody else, I am on my*

own journey for understanding and still have a long way
to go. Also, like most of us, I have suffered loss in my life,
but two things really keep making it extremely difficult
for me to overcome and move into the future with a hap-
pier outlook. I would dearly love to have some connection
with those who have passed and have had nothing. Is
that because they do not love on the same scale I do?
Also, last year I had to undergo pretty extensive surgery.
It set off "panic syndrome." I had always thought that I
was a believer and was shaken that when the crunch
came I was just a big bowl of jelly. All in all this has not
been a bad thing as it has sent me down this path in
search of light. Well, what I'm trying to say is, George, do
you think it's a lack of faith or love on my part that I feel
so disconnected and so totally alone? Many thanks.

—*Jane*

Dianne Arcangel, which, quite interestingly, is her actual name, has been a dear friend of mine for many years, from as far back as when she was working as a researcher with Dr. Elisabeth Kübler-Ross and Dr. Raymond Moody— two pioneers in the study of spontaneous apparitions.

When I met Dianne, she was a dyed-in-the-wool skeptic of mediumship, having seen too much fraud and not enough empirical evidence, both as a scientist and as a human being. So when it came to meeting me, she put me through my paces during a session she had with me. Although I always find satisfaction in turning the head of a skeptical researcher, I found something more valuable in Dianne's approval of my ability. She was able to take it and use it to help forward many of her theories about life hereafter and the presence of the souls in people's lives. Dianne has spent the better part of her career studying spontaneous apparitions—visitations from the souls to friends and family members, unassisted by mediumship, a dream state, or any other device. Her book, *Afterlife Encounters*, shows her evidence culled from thousands of spontaneous apparitions from people all over the country and the world.

One thing I found most interesting when I met Dianne was that as a researcher things must be proven to her with evidence that will hold up to scrutiny. But as a human being, there seemed to be a part of Dianne that was exhausted from promises made by psychics and mediums about their supposed ability to contact those who have passed. Hearing actual communication from loved ones in her life seemed to jump-start her sleeping belief and propel her toward new goals in her own research.

Similarly, I believe Jane's faith has fallen asleep—it seems to be there, but hidden somehow under disbelief and what I can only describe as "exhaustion"—a clear need to believe, but also a palpable absence of real answers that has the potential to leave us weak and unfeeling when we most need to believe. It is very common among people who are struggling to make some sense out of their lives and their faith, only to see no real light ahead of them to which they can point their beliefs. We become exhausted from too many questions and not enough evidence to support our beliefs. Nearly everyone I meet who feels let down not only by life, but by life hereafter, feels very much abandoned by the prospect of hope. In this case, it will be up to us to find it, rebuild it, and trust it again.

Things that go on in our lives will begin to chip away at our hope, usually at the very time we need to count on it. It has happened to each of us, in different times in our lives, and it seems inescapable. But just when we think we have been forgotten by a world that was supposed to continue caring for us, something happens that will change everything. The only problem is that before the souls can change anything for us, we have to change everything within ourselves that makes us think we have, for even one second, been cast aside or forgotten by those who are cheering and pulling for us every day—the souls.

Let's start with a change of attitude by pointing out the obvious—we are never alone on the earth when we have a loved one in the hereafter. They care for us in ways that may not seem measurable to us, but they have been happening all along. Proof of that can be found in Jane's letter. She mentioned being frightened, but what changed? Where did she find the strength to go forward with her surgery? Something within Jane made her understand that it all would come out all right, and she listened to the voice within and went ahead, even being frightened. That is the awakening of faith.

One of the most popular signs I see from the souls in sessions who want to explain more about our faith is the showing of the final scene of the movie *The Wizard of Oz*, in which Dorothy finds out that she had the power to go home any time she wanted, but she had to find it for herself. The souls use this very definitive symbol to teach each of us that no one can hand you faith—it must be found within you, and you must allow it to grow without hovering too much and smothering its growth. The signs are much bigger than we think—just as Dorothy's ruby slippers should have been the biggest sign that something around her had intense power. We pass the signs of light that are all around us because we don't recognize them for what they actually are—symbols from the souls who have been by our side from nearly the moment of our own journey here. But we don't see them because we don't know how to look at them.

I tell many of my clients who have told me about their "lack" of signs to look much closer. Nothing is ever going to be as big as a burning bush, unless the souls know it is something we can understand and handle. Those lucky enough to have had a full-on apparition of their loved ones earned it—by finding first the small signs, and accepting without question that the possibility of their loved ones just showing themselves and speaking words of peace to them is absolutely attainable. And it happens, just like that. The issue is not that we don't believe hard enough in the souls, the issue is more that we don't believe hard enough in ourselves—in our own faith and in our own hope. This is something very easy to change—it just requires looking at the world and the road we are on in a much more detailed and careful way.

I will be the first one to tell you that not everything we go through is a mystical experience. But some things are unmistakable—kindness from a complete stranger when we felt our most alone; issues we were so worried about somehow resolving themselves without too much of our own work; and even me pulling Jane's letter from a box of hundreds that wanted a personal answer to some difficult questions. These are not random or coincidental—there is a definite method to the madness here. The steps seem small, I will agree, but the more we believe in those first small steps, the bigger the steps get, and the more profound the signs we receive will become. Faith is a funny thing—we actually have to give some to get some. And it all starts with a fundamental belief: No matter how small the signs, even if they seem nonexistent to us, we are loved by those who have passed before us into the world hereafter. They love us because they understand us in a way they never could have on the earth—to our very heart and soul. They want to make a difference in our lives, but they have the very careful balancing act of keeping our faith alive without taking our lessons from us and extinguishing the fire we need to continue. We need to show the souls we believe in them, and they will respond in kind by showing us in so many ways how much they believe in us.

We need not worry about faith—it never leaves you. Just like Dorothy's slippers, the power of faith has been with us all the time, even if we did not recognize it. We have more of a connection to the souls than we realize, and they are walking with us, even when we cannot feel them. I tell people in sessions that I cannot prove 100 percent that their loved ones are communicating, because the souls will never prove to me 100 percent that they are—that part is left to us to figure out as a matter of faith. Nobody can hand faith to us, because it is part of what we must learn while we are on the earth. But look around you—the signs are everywhere, if not subtle and easy to overlook. The souls are there, and they always have been. And they always will be. Don't ask the souls to prove to you that they believe in you—instead, show the souls that you have faith in them, and they will reward your faith with signs that will help you understand just how much you are cared for, even when you think you are alone. Look for the signs—they are rather like a beacon in the distance: At first, small and seemingly so far away, but as we believe and walk toward them, they become bigger and brighter. Soon, with our faith intact, we can live in the light that beacon of hope casts over us, and we can continue our journey here, knowing always that we are loved, we are cared for, and that we are never alone on the earth.

CHAPTER EIGHT

What Are You Doing the Rest of Your Life?

Dear George:

I was listening to your session, and I'm curious what the souls tell you about why it is so important for us to live on, especially considering how much we suffer here? Why should we not be in a hurry to join the souls in the hereafter?

—Melody

Early on in this book, I mentioned my fascination with television as a young boy growing up in the 1950s. Although I know I will place myself squarely in the "over the hill" category when I say this, one of the things I always found so prevalent in the television shows I used to watch was a rather old-fashioned notion that you can never get something for nothing. I would watch, rapt, as Ralph Kramden in *The Honeymooners* tried so hard to put some of his harebrained, get-rich-quick schemes into play, only to fail miserably, because, as the myriad of people watching that small black-and-white box already knew, you cannot get something for nothing, and riches cannot come to people who do not work for them.

In the world we live in now, with things going lightning speed, start-up companies and Internet programs that can spring up suddenly and garner millions of dollars, I think much of that simple ethic has been lost. However, it may have been lost to the people of the earth, but it has never been lost to the souls. The only way we can create a world of peace, joy, and happiness for ourselves in the world hereafter is to build it brick by brick, day by day, and struggle by struggle. There is no easy way to earn the joy and beauty of the world hereafter if we do not do the work here that is required of us. Just like the harebrained schemes of 1950s television, they are a house of sand. We might be able to fool others into thinking we have earned something when we didn't, but we certainly can never fool ourselves, the souls or the world hereafter.

We come to the earth with a definitive plan—a road map that will be our life's work on the earth. This plan not only affects our journey here, but the journey of each of the people whose lives we impact with our own. Each of us struggles, we learn, we fall, we learn again, and we continue. We try to complete the lessons we have given ourselves, for good or for bad, but no matter what we do here, just *trying* to stick to the road map is also one of our biggest lessons here. Many of the struggles have been built in to our lesson, and others arise as a result of our varied success at what we tried to achieve here—whether we chose compassion over judgment, kindness over cruelty, and honesty over duplicity. Each of these things provides a solid foundation from which the monument to our existence here springs up, and it gives us the opportunity to continue on to a world we have built for ourselves in a place far more beautiful and easy, where those who have already struggled, learned, and have overcome their life lessons find the peace and joy they now truly deserve.

We cannot be in a hurry to have something we did not earn, because there are no easy shortcuts to our lives here. The souls have proven that many times, by telling us that whatever is not finished on the earth must be finished in the hereafter. Although the hereafter is a much easier place to learn and grow, the souls tell us constantly that *here* is where the learning needs to be—we have the time, we have the resolve, and we have the ability. The souls who worked hard all their lives, and struggled through whatever was thrown in their path understand this the most. In looking back at the earth, they are proud of their accomplishments, and they are happy to have made a dent in the minds and hearts of people still on the earth with their own acts of kindness, compassion, and faith. There is a great amount of satisfaction among the souls at a job well done—they earned the right to live in a world that is now free of struggle, and they implore each of us to stick to our plan here, finish, learn what we can, and earn the right to move on, just as they did. Every second, they tell us, is worth it. That's a rather big statement to make, considering how many of the souls truly suffered and struggled on the earth. But still, they tell us, every second of the pain, every second of the struggle, and every second they spent making a better life for themselves paid off so handsomely for them in the world hereafter that they would gladly do it all again to achieve the same result. It is so profound a statement that we have to believe them and take them at their word.

None of the struggles we face here are easy, but all of them are necessary. The souls want us to do the best we can to continue learning and growing on the earth, experiencing and understanding, falling and getting back up—all so that we can also build a beautiful world for ourselves with our hard work and faith. It may not ever make complete sense while we are here, but the souls promise it will make perfect sense when we see the fruits of our struggle blossom for us after all our work here is done. Continue living and learning here—every second of it will pay off for you in a world to come.

Dear George:

I am almost ashamed to write to you, knowing that you deal with people in great amounts of pain who are strug-

gling every day just to hold on to their sanity. But I know
that you have had clients come, and have spoken to the
souls from just about every walk of life, from the terribly
poor to the very rich and famous. I am hoping they may
have some advice for me. I have been very fortunate in
my life, but I feel as if I am not doing what I was meant
to be doing in my life. I have everything I need, but some-
how I feel empty. It feels like I should be doing more, and
I feel restless. Is there anything that the spirits suggest we
concentrate on while we are here, to really make an
impact on the earth?

—*Vince*

Feeling restless and having the wherewithal to do more in
your life is one of the happier struggles we will have here,
but it is also just as important and valuable as some of the
more difficult struggles some of us may face. I always believe
that when things come to a calm point in our journey here,
something within us makes us start looking for *more*—more
ways to help others on the earth, and more ways to bring caring and compassion to those who truly need it. It is also helpful for people to know that not every life lesson is borne out
of fear and pain. Sometimes people are chosen to help others
from a very fortunate place in their own lives, and the value
of their contributions to a world of those in need cannot ever
be measured. But they will always be recognized by the souls,
and counted among our greatest achievements here.

Many people who know me know my fondness for St. Katharine Drexel. She was born in 1858, into a very wealthy and privileged banking family. Instead of living a life of leisure like many of the Philadelphia socialites of her day, St. Katharine became restless and saddened by the racial intolerance she saw around her, especially with regard to Native Americans and African Americans. She decided to use her family's name and vast inheritance to create and finance more than sixty missions and schools around the United States, as well as founding the Order of the Sisters of the Blessed Sacrament. She was canonized in 2000 by Pope John Paul II, and her efforts to eradicate social inequality among minorities continues to this day. Although she grew up in a very comfortable circumstance, she was certainly no stranger to hard work, and her concern for those living in poverty and isolation due to their ethnic backgrounds has impacted the lives of so many people.

St. Katharine was living proof that where we start in our journey is not as important as where we *go* in it. To take whatever we have, no matter how little or how much, and use it to help change the world around us is one of the greatest gifts we can give the earth. Each of us has the ability to change the lives and the circumstances of those around us, and it takes neither money nor privilege—it only takes the desire to want to make a difference in the lives of people who can use our help. There are so many resources that can use your hands, your mind, and your heart, that the possibilities are nearly endless. Consider volunteering your time helping those who truly need it the most—in an animal shelter, or in a homeless shelter, in soup kitchens or any kind of mission that needs hands and hearts more than they need money. The greatest gift we can give anyone is our time, our compassion, and our inclination to help when it is needed. You may never see the immediate results of your hard work on the earth, but trust me that every second spent helping another on the earth who is going through struggle is registered and counted, not only by those who were fortunate to be the beneficiary of your hard work and kindness, but by the souls, who understand how important this kind of work is on the earth.

Dear George:

I have an overwhelming desire to help parents who have lost a child. How can I do that? What should I do? I think I have (finally) accepted my son Adam's death, but there are times that I'm not sure I have. So, am I in a position to help others? What would Adam want me to do? I'm sorry for "pestering" but your words are so comforting. Thank you, George.

—Cathi

I must tell you that I get goose bumps from letters like this one. To find people so willing to share their hope in the midst of their pain is the very essence of what the souls tell us our life lesson is all about. The fact that Cathi can even consider someone outside of herself who is experiencing the same pain, and wants to help, says a lot about the success of her journey here, and how well she has come to grow from the hard struggles she was presented with.

I've often told parents who have lost a child that if they wanted to see their child's eventual work on the earth, to hold up their own two hands. Why? Because *we* have the power to continue the memory of their lifetime here by honoring them with work they would have been proud to do themselves. Anything we do in a loved one's name honors their memory, and keeps them alive in the hearts of whoever benefits from your good work. I find that there is a real beauty in people who have experienced such heartache and suffering, especially after the loss of a child, who want to reach out to others, in order to make the very difficult road just a bit easier to navigate. It's an amazing gift.

Parents who have lost a child are in the most unique and experienced position to help another parent who is struggling through crisis right now. They have been there, have lived through the terror, and have learned through both faith and sheer will that time does heal wounds, and that everything that happens to us in this lifetime does truly have a purpose. It is a very difficult thing for someone to ponder in those first few terrible minutes, hours, and days after loss, but it is important and necessary to learn as quickly as possible. People will respond to you a lot faster and recognize your achievement because you were once a student of loss, and now you can become a teacher of hope in a life that may be hard-pressed to find any reason to continue hoping. People in a grief situation look to others in the same boat, because they want to know some things that are so basic, only somebody who has truly been in their shoes can understand: How do you get up the next morning and continue your life? How do you explain your inability to recover to friends and family? What do you tell people who tell you to "move on" when you can't? These are questions only somebody who has lived through it and came out the other side of hope can answer with honesty.

I have found in my own career that people respond much better to frankness and candor than they do to sugarcoated words and platitudes. Like my father used to say, "Fancy words don't put food on the table," and it certainly doesn't serve anyone who needs practical advice on just staying *alive*, both physically and emotionally, after the passing of a child. People who have been through the same ordeal are a wellspring of experience and advice that anyone would be proud to learn from. And there is an added benefit to helping those in the same circumstance as yourself—you honor those you love, who continue to help you to find the right words to tell others. Knowing that you are bringing comfort and a real understanding of what it means to be bereaved brings each of us closer to those we love who have passed, because they stay close to us, to keep us upright and able to help those who need it more than we do. There will always be times when your own loss may overwhelm you, but knowing that you found a way to reach out to another in the same position will have a sense of purpose and reward to it. I could not think of a better way to honor the lives of those we love than to take whatever hope we have managed to scrape up after a difficult time, and toss it in the direction of all those who need it just a little more. The souls have told me that at the very time we are so generous as to give away what little we have, it comes back to us in ways that may surprise and astound us. The best way to create hope in ourselves is to freely give it away to others—it will always come back to us and see us through the rest of our journey here.

Cathi is the best example of hope another bereaved parent could wish for, and she is the best example of peace and growth the souls could ever want for us. I congratulate her for taking the first step on the road to a completely fulfilled journey here.

Dear George:

The physicist Stephen Hawking recently said that the afterlife and Heaven is a "fairy" story for people afraid of dying. You obviously don't believe that, but in all your work you must come across a lot of skeptics. What would your answer to him be?

—Anthony

This may surprise a lot of people, but I completely understand Mr. Hawking's comment, and in an odd way, I have to agree with it—to a point. But we need to remember that what seems like a drop of brilliance in comprehension about only one point will still disappear in a sea of total understanding when we finally see the big picture. Like the souls who talk about religion, and say that each has a facet but none has the entire diamond, I do believe that Mr. Hawking does hold one facet of a very important point about faith, our need to believe, and just what exactly it is we think we are supposed to believe.

Most of us know that Stephen Hawking, a world-renown physicist and the Director of Research at the Center of Theoretical Cosmology at Cambridge University, has also lived a life of struggle and difficulty, having been diagnosed with Lou Gehrig's Disease (ALS) at the age of twenty-one years old. As a scientist, his work in discovering the eleven dimensions of the universe has been able to show many of us that there are things around us we may never have been able to understand but for dedicated research and compelling evidence to support the claims. Mr. Hawking deals in a world of absolutes, but must concede that much of his work rests in the theoretical—meaning that his work is based in *theory* rather than practical application. We cannot measure the dimensions of the universe, or see them, or even feel them. But Mr. Hawking, with his brilliant mind, can come to his conclusions based on everything he knows will lead us to the same theory, based on everything he has learned.

This is where his point both comes together and falls apart. I also believe that most of what we are taught about "Heaven" or the world hereafter is a fairy tale. It is often cringe-inducing for me to hear people explain "Heaven" as a place where an old man sits on a throne, judging us as to our worthiness, casting some of us to eternal fires of unhappiness, and others a place at his right hand. It has all the makings of a first-class fairy tale, and not one word of it is the truth. It is stunning, however, how many people believe just that. We have no proof whatsoever that this world exists, except in the minds of those who espouse a particular religion, and that religion happens to be the largest on the earth. But truth isn't decided by majority rule, so in many ways, I have to agree with Mr. Hawking that the story in its entirety is a fairy tale.

I have explained how I feel his theory comes together, and now I will try to explain why I feel it falls apart at the very same time. Mr. Hawking bases his own work on *theory*— empirical data that leads us to the most likely conclusion. In that same vein, I, and everyone who has ever had a visitation from the souls can be considered a theoretical physicist—we have seen the empirical evidence with our own eyes, our own ears, and our own hearts, so it is no longer possible to put that genie back in the bottle. We *know* there is a hereafter; a fairy tale can't produce the kind of communication and involvement with the earth that the souls have shown so many of us over the years. So we have to play the part of the physicist, gather up our evidence—years and years of proof that the souls have communicated—and come to our conclusion that there is, in fact, a hereafter—perhaps the twelfth of Mr. Hawking's eleven dimensions of the universe.

Another problem with Mr. Hawking's assessment of "Heaven" or the world hereafter is that his argument that the mind simply "switches off like a broken-down computer when we die" has already been proven to be hopelessly inaccurate. Studies have already shown that our consciousness continues in spite of our physical bodies, and continues through the universe because it is *energy*, and energy does not die. Researchers like Dr. Kenneth Ring and Dr. Gary Schwartz have devoted the better part of their lives in the hopes of showing people that consciousness does not die, no matter what happens to the physical body. Once considered only the domain of fringe-science, more in the medical and scientific community have latched onto this premise, based in part by the number of thoroughly researched Near Death Experiences which have proven that even though the body ceases to exist, even for a short amount of time, the consciousness stays alive. Although I think it's wonderful that we have more scientific study on which to rely, it is nothing more than what the souls have been telling us, in one way or another, about their life and the world hereafter. Once again, everything old becomes new again.

I'm actually amazed at the controversy Mr. Hawking's statements have caused, especially among the religious communities. It makes me wonder why, if we build our religion on faith, it is so fragile that it cannot hold up under the weight of an alternate and contrary opinion? People have told me quite frequently all through my life that they think the concept of being able to "hear from the dead" is impossible, and that I cannot do what I claim. To me, the statement has no ability to anger me or weaken my belief in the souls, and for a very simple reason: *I can see and hear them.* To me, it seems as silly as telling you that you cannot read the sentence you are reading right at this moment. Where is the anger coming from when people hear a contrary opinion, and why isn't their belief strong enough to withstand any scrutiny? I've spent the better part of my early career trying to put my money where my mouth is by allowing myself to be subjected to just about every test the researchers could come up with to prove my ability. To this day, I am the most tested medium of this lifetime, and although that sounds like quite an achievement, the best the researchers have ever been able to do is scratch their heads, because they know *something* is going on when I discern the souls—they just can't or won't say what.

I am very glad for the Stephen Hawkings of the world. One of the things Mr. Hawking did say in an interview, even though he was disputing the notion of life after death, was that each of us needs to "fulfill our own potential by making good use of our lives while we are here." A truer statement will never be made. *Here* is where the proving ground is, and here is where we will have our most shining moments of achievement—if we can think of our journey on the earth as having a specific purpose, as well as a beginning, an end, and a reward for having lived here. But another reason why I am glad for people like Mr. Hawking is that they teach us to really look at what we believe and *why*. It simply isn't good enough that we believe without reservation everything we are told, simply because most people believe it. When I set out to write books on the subject of the souls and the world hereafter, I try to come from a place in my own belief, and simply place it in front of the reader for him or her to make up their own mind, based on what I have been able to present, and how compelling they find the evidence. At the end of the day, each of us must decide for ourselves what it is that makes up our belief and our faith, and it should be something nobody can shake from us, especially not with simply a theory to the contrary. My belief, and the belief of those everywhere on earth who have been witness to the incredible experience of having seen, heard or spoken to the souls is something that is life-altering, and cannot be shaken from them, no matter how hard the skeptics try. Once you see that the sky is blue, it is simply impossible to believe it is green, no matter what evidence is presented to the contrary. Our theories are what we learn from in life, but our beliefs are truly who we *are* and who we aspire to be.

Dear George:

Why does it take going through really difficult times for us to search for more meaning in our lives? Even as a child, I knew there must be more to life than what I knew.

*Too bad we don't live our lives knowing the true meaning
of why we are here much sooner. I think we would all be
much happier knowing what we have in store for us when
we cross over.*

—Kelly

I am a big believer that ignorance is the only true bliss there
is to be found on the earth. I think if we actually knew
how bumpy the road would be here, we would have never
signed on. But here we are, having decided before we came
to the earth that we had some specific and difficult lessons
to learn, and here we also are, struggling to understand,
cope, and continue moving forward.

I don't think it's possible for us to know what our journey
would be on the earth, and for a few reasons. Firstly, I don't
think we would have picked up the gauntlet, knowing how
heavy it would be in advance. Secondly, I don't believe we
would have been able to make the important decisions we
need to make, especially if we came to understand in advance
the impact those decisions would have on our lives and the
lives of those around us. And lastly, I know, because the souls
have told me repeatedly, that if we knew in advance the
answers to the world here, it would certainly not be a test of
our courage, our faith, and our will.

Conversely, if we knew exactly what we were to receive
in the hereafter for any specific struggle we had on the earth,
how hard would we try to actually resolve these issues and

try to live our best possible lives? Many people have written me over the years asking why we need to face the challenges we face, if the world hereafter holds no judgment, has no recourse for a failed journey, and life there is perfect and beautiful no matter what we do or how badly we fall off our spiritual path. The answer to that is actually even more simple: *We* know. We are the only ones who will judge what we have or haven't done on the earth, and we are the soul arbiter of just what kind of reward we deserve for having worked hard, or not, while we were on the earth. And the souls know just how hard a judge each of us, in complete and utter honesty, can be with ourselves.

When I was very young, the priest from our church asked me and my brother to clean out the basement of the rectory. It was a bit of a dusty mess with plenty of old furniture and debris packed down there, but we were promised fifty cents apiece for our efforts—enough money to send us running with brooms and pails to the rectory basement.

But what began in earnest turned slowly into a need to sit on an orange crate, then to ponder what wonderful things could be bought for half a dollar, and then to the most cursory of efforts to sweep dust into corners, arrange some boxes and chairs, and call it a day.

When we felt we were finished, we went back to the priest, who smiled and honored his obligation by giving each of us a shiny new Kennedy half-dollar coin. I saw the lovely coin, and nearly put it into my pocket, until I was struck with guilt. "Didn't you want to see the basement first?" I asked him, while my brother glared at me from behind the priest's shoulder. "That's not necessary," he said, smiling. "You know what kind of job you did." My brother and I put the coins in our pockets, returned to the basement, and emerged three hours later, covered in dirt, but proud of having earned not only the coin, but the trust that was freely given with it.

Sometimes it's best not to know the *whys* or *hows* of the things we must endure while we are on the earth, because it may derail us from perhaps some of the most important lessons we will learn on the earth, because we would only find easy ways out of the circumstances we know we must face. But because we will be our only judge, and the only one we will eventually have to be completely honest with, we know we have to do the work required of us, or it will all be for naught.

I think we really do know why we are here, what we are here to learn, and what we have in store for us if we can only stay the course and complete what we have set out for ourselves. We may not be aware completely of the twists and turns that will occur on a frequently changing path, but we do understand that we are here to face the challenges we have created for ourselves, and complete them to the very best of our abilities. We, each of us, can be the people we know are within us, and the souls know also. They ask us to "be the people we know you already are." It is an amazing statement, because the souls see and understand us at our very core—without having to check to see what kind of job we are capable of. They see our capacity to love, our ability to forgive, and the strength within each of us that keeps us going, in spite of setbacks and obstacles. It's an indicator of how much we are loved, how much we are trusted, and how much can be expected of us—not only by the souls, but by ourselves. The meaning and purpose in our lives endure because *we* endure—we will always be able to face what we thought we could never face, and overcome everything we thought could never be overcome. The souls believe in us and trust in us, and we have to take that belief and trust, and turn it into accomplishments. Only then will we see the panorama of the meaning of our lives unfold for us—when the work is done, and when we are able to pick up that shiny coin and put it proudly in our pocket.

Dear George:

How can I help my mother? She has terminal cancer and does not talk about it very much. I want to help her through this as best as I can. She knows I took my father's death badly in 2006. But I will be strong for her, if only she will let me. George, your books have gotten me through some very tough times and I thank you.

—Trish

Those who are ready to make the transition are more afraid for us than they are for themselves. They just need reassurance. My mother, twenty-four hours before her own passing, insisted that the hospice call me because she had a question. She asked me if it was okay to go, and I told her yes—that my dad needed her there more than I needed her here. Somehow that's all she needed to know.

People who are nearing the end of their physical life on the earth begin to worry that they will have no more connection with those who will be left behind. They fear an inability to be able to care for their children in a way every parent wants to care for their children, no matter what age they are. It is part of our human nature to fear what we don't yet understand, but in many sessions I have done for people who are facing imminent passing, the souls have been at their most compassionate and practical regarding the connection the souls have with the earth, and how the connection from mother to child, from hereafter to here, can never be broken.

It's often funny and poignant to hear the souls in a session become cheerleaders and de facto tour guides for those whose passing is just a matter of time. They really go all out to help not only the one who is nearing their passing, but also family members who are unsure what to expect when their loved one faces those few moments on the earth. A few years ago we received a call from the wife of a man who was terminally ill, and already in the hospital with almost no time left. His prognosis was very poor, and doctors had asked the family to get their affairs in order quickly, while the husband and father of three was still lucid. When the wife called, she simply wanted advice as to how best to help her husband through his transition, and how best to explain it to their young children, who had to bear witness to their father's difficult ordeal. Within two hours of the phone call, we arranged for me to come and just sit with the family awhile, and let them decide whether or not a session was in order.

I was rather surprised how much the husband wanted to hear from his own loved ones in the hereafter; it was pretty clear to me that he was scared. I wondered if my presence would spook him even more, but oddly, he found comfort in knowing that we cared enough to visit him and be whatever help we could be. He decided to have a session, and asked if his children could be present. I always know that having children at a session is a very constructive and helpful part of the grief process, because at the very least, it opens up dialogue that will put their father's life in the future, and not in the past.

Immediately in the session, the man's parents came through, and told him they were waiting, and that if he looked carefully enough, he would know when the time was that he would be leaving the earth, because he would see the portal open, and be able to see his family, friends, and pets lined up on the other side to greet him and encourage him to walk through. They talked about the kind of world he would live in, what he might do, and how he would be able to communicate to his wife and children in a way that is so much closer than any parent could be to a child on the earth. I found it very poignant to hear the man's mother tell him that he could be a better father to his children from the hereafter than he ever could have been on the earth, because no matter where they went, no matter how old and independent they got, he would always live in their hearts, and they would carry him everywhere. I know that by the end of the session, he had found some peace and comfort, and the children, now understanding exactly where their father would be headed, lost a little of the fear they had about losing him to his illness. Sometimes all we need is the assurance that we will never be forgotten by those still on the earth, and that we still have the power to be a force of love in their lives.

Here is what I would tell Trish to do for her mother: Tell your mom that you love her enough to send her to her glory and reward. Make an imaginary rope, and "hand" her one end, and "tie" the other to your wrist. Let her know that you will never drop your end of the rope, and that she has to promise never to let go of her end. Mothers always need to feel like mothers, even when their job is done. Let her know that she can do more for you in the hereafter than she can do on the earth, and that the "rope" you both hold will always connect you. Make her promise she'll help you from the hereafter, and she'll know she'll still have a job to do for you when she gets there. Knowing that she can still take care of you from the hereafter will help her understand that the transition is only a change of physical presence, and that love will always connect you both. And you will also know that you are connected to both parents in a way that transcends time and space—you have the "rope" which binds you to prove it.

Dear George:

Where do we find the strength to continue on when life has gotten the better of us?

—Maria

This question is both simple and complex at the same time, because depending on which direction you approach it, it will have very different answers. It would be very easy to pull out an expression from my drawerful of pat answers, like "Let your faith be your guide," but somehow, I feel there is more in this question than the words are actually saying.

There is something I like to call the *five-year syndrome,* and because I work mostly with the bereaved, it has come to symbolize bereavement, although it can apply to anything that happens in our lifetime that it will take months and perhaps years to recover from—the loss of a loved one, the loss of a job, the loss of our hope, or the loss of the will to continue fighting on the earth. The *five-year syndrome* is something I have noticed that happens to people who have experienced a profound loss in their lifetime, chronic illness, or depression from a series of difficult circumstances—right around the five-year mark, hope seems to vaporize, faith seems to depart, and people get *tired*. They get tired of being different, or sick, or bereaved, or anything else that takes them out of the ordinary, especially within their circle of friends and family. People who have gone through major, difficult circumstances just want their lives to be *normal* again, and they don't want to be defined by their circumstance any longer.

I've seen some pretty awful things happen when people feel like they have been exhausted, physically, mentally, and emotionally by their strained circumstances. Marriages fall apart, friendships disintegrate, and people pull away from the very resources they desperately need to continue learning and growing. This is a critical point in the lives of each of us who are facing difficult, ongoing challenges, and unless we are willing to step outside everything we ever believed about ourselves and our own lives, we have no choice but to be swallowed up by our own self-pity, and cast adrift by our own hopelessness. I still can't know for sure whether people come to this realization that *everything* must change, or if that thought is mercifully placed in our heads and hearts by the souls, but those who truly survive to continue another day, another week, another year on their journey have to leave the life they once knew, and everything with it, behind. They have to begin thinking of a new life—a second chapter in a story that still has a few surprises left for each of us, if we allow ourselves to completely reinvent our reasons for being on the earth, and the circumstances that brought us to where we find ourselves now.

There are very few stories of hope that I find so remarkable that I want to tell the story to everybody I know who is in pain, because they so perfectly illustrate what the souls have been trying to tell us about rethinking everything we know about our journey here, when we feel we have no place else to go. In a sink or swim situation, I am always so dumbstruck at the human courage people have to *swim* when it would have been so much easier just to sink. Not only do people like this learn to swim, but they find the courage to *fly*—to take their circumstances and change the world with the force of their convictions, and their hearts full of hope.

I met Robin Stein when she came for a session a few years ago under an assumed name. It was perhaps the smartest thing she did, because the circumstances of her son Morris's passing were newsworthy, and the reports of his passing were in many of the South Florida papers and television news.

Morris Stein was nineteen years old and attending Tallahassee Community College, some distance away from his mom, with whom he shared a very close mother-and-son, but also a loving "buddy-style" relationship. Although it was hard for Robin, a single mom and an easygoing free spirit, to let her only son go away to college, she knew he would do well for himself, and his best friend as his roommate in Tallahassee would ensure that Morris wouldn't be lonely in a new town and in a new environment.

The boys took a trip to a gun show in December of that year, where each of them purchased a gun—something they had never owned before. While Morris's friend purchased a shotgun, Morris was an environmentalist and animal lover, so the gun he purchased was more trophy than weapon—an antique French rifle. The two bonded even closer over their newfound hobby, having gone a few times to the shooting range in the forest to practice their skills and perfect their aim.

On January 17, 2008, Morris's friend was unaware that Morris was in the apartment at the time he took out his shotgun to admire. He thought the safety was in place, but then Morris, who was in fact home at the time, rounded the corner of his friend's room, and in a terrible flash, the gun went off, hitting Morris in the chest. Morris fell to the ground and although he struggled to say alive, Morris died of a single gunshot wound shortly afterward.

This is the part of the story where someone like Robin would come for a session, the souls would speak and try to bring some comfort and peace, and then they would go home, become bereaved, and do their best to deal, for the rest of their lives. But Robin is not an ordinary woman, and what she has done to honor the life of her son, Morris, has had wide and lasting implications, not only in the lives of others, but in the sparing of yet another life. A year later, Robin was already honoring the memory of her son by beginning a petition and campaign to teach young people how to safely handle firearms. With the help of other parents of the close-knit community in which she lives, she created the MoSt Foundation (the first two letters of Morris's first and last name,) with its mission to "make the world we live in a better place by encouraging individual responsibility and fostering awareness of ways to take responsibility." The foundation has already garnered attention and made strides within the community, but what Robin would do next forced her completely out of the box of her grief, and into a place where she could literally alter the life circumstance of another human being also facing tragedy and despair—the boy who shot her son.

It takes a special place in each of us to find forgiveness for a person who has done harm to someone we love, but it also takes a belief in wanting to triumph in the life lessons that are placed before us, to want to go above and beyond our own pain to do something so extraordinary, it is a symbol to me of the grace of the souls and the power of the Infinite Light within each of us to do the right thing. Robin knew with all her heart that the boy who shot her son did so accidentally, and that he truly loved her son. But the shooting was a matter of the Leon County Prosecutor's Office, who filed charges of manslaughter against the teen—a charge that carried with it the possibility of fifteen years in jail for the nineteen-year-old who accidentally killed his best friend.

After the deliberation phase of the manslaughter trial against the boy who shot her son, Robin did something that changed the course of her own grief journey, and perhaps the life lessons of both the boy, his family, and anyone who was privileged to witness her actions. She stood in front of the judge and pleaded for leniency for the boy who killed her son. While others, like Morris's father, demanded a manslaughter conviction, Robin understood that Morris would have never wanted his good friend to go down the terrible road of incarceration and ruin the rest of his life because of a senseless accident. She simply did what came from within her heart—she told the judge, "I don't think this child will survive jail. I don't think he's going to go a day in his life without dealing with what happened. I don't think he should spend a night in jail—he won't survive it. He'll kill himself. He loved my son, and my son loved him, and they were stupid," before collapsing into tears.

The moment that we face our lives, and we face everything we thought we had known, and begin to see the world the way the souls have always envisioned it, brings us to a place of such clarity and peace that we know we have forever altered the way we will continue through the rest of our journey here. It will also forever change the way others will see what true hope in the face of such despair really means. As a result of her moving statement, Morris's friend was given a greatly reduced sentence.

There are few times in my life where I have been able to witness the presence of the Infinite Light's work on the earth—where even the most impossible of circumstances become possible, and a life that looked so dark suddenly fills with light. The story of Robin's willingness to put her own grief and pain aside and find a reason to look for a bigger purpose than just her own journey is a testament of just how much we can move on from our pain, our suffering, and our feeling of being stuck in circumstances that seem to have no way out. Our willingness to follow the path of the souls and our firm belief that good can be found, no matter how difficult the struggle, is our way out of the shackles of pain and suffering to finding a reason to look toward light. We need more Robin Steins on the earth—we need more examples of impossible, improbable hope to marvel at when we feel everything is coming down for us. Sometimes, just looking past our own struggles, and to the very reason why we are here, brings us to a place of understanding where doubt and fear about the road up ahead will never touch us again. We can only hope, but we can always try.

It Was All So Beautiful

Perception is a funny thing—what we see is not always what we get. Take the sky, for instance. It's easy enough to look upward and see a clear blue sky. At least that's what we *think* we see. I remember, as a student at Our Lady of Perpetual Help High School, when we were herded into the gymnasium to sit in front of a large television, and watch the Apollo 7 crew launch its way into the sky on October 11, 1968. I remember watching the sky go from light blue, to deep blue, to black as the rocket propelled itself toward space. That's when I began to realize that the sky may not, in fact, be blue at all. It's only our perception, from where we are standing on the earth, that makes it blue.

I find myself thinking back to that revelation whenever I speak to people who find themselves at a crossroads on the earth, whether through loss, financial hardship, a changing world or an inability to cope with circumstances that have gone beyond their control. Their world, their issues, and their struggles are a matter of perception, at least to me. They know I speak to the souls, they know the souls speak about their beautiful world, and yet, to many people, the souls and the prospect of a world hereafter are only a concept. What I perceive as blue, they perceive as black. No matter what we are told, no matter what we come to understand, the struggles we live through and the issues we will face are only problems in our own world. But are we looking carefully enough at the concept of our struggles, or are we so grounded on the earth that we can't see from another perspective that what we have come to understand may not be everything we know?

I've been trained over the years, mostly by the souls, to look at the world from my vantage point, but also the vantage point of the souls. Where we see loss, the souls see gain— they have gone to a beautiful world, and gained reward for having struggled on the earth. They took that trip through the atmosphere just as the astronauts took their trip to a whole new level of understanding. For the souls, their perspective about everything on the earth has changed— mainly because they can see it from a better perspective—they are *there*. They see the earth now much the same as we see images of the earth from space—remote, undaunting, serene, beautiful, and *small*. They see their new world as vast, open, filled with possibilities, unending, yet still linked to the world, the people, and the lives they knew.

Even with everything we know, with everything we've been taught about the world hereafter and the souls—about their ability to live, love, struggle, cope, and continue through this lifetime and their exit to a world of joy—we still see our own temporary state of affairs here as something terrible, unforgiving, and unending. It happens because perceptions are hard to change, and old ways of thinking are hard to break.

So how do we change our perception of our lives and struggles on the earth, and try to see from the perspective the souls see? It begins with seeing ourselves as "souls in training." Astronauts, before they delve into space, rely on simulators to help them adapt to the changes they will experience once they get into space. How I wish we had a program here to help us understand the transition our loved ones go through, by simulating a beautiful world, filled with joy and peace. But it's not ours to have, just yet. We have to try to understand from everything the souls have told us about their world, and try to imagine the life those who have also navigated the earth now live. It's not easy—our world is filled with pain, especially in the painful lessons we endure, and it's filled with more questions than answers. In a way, each of us has to create our own "flight simulator"—to imagine those who have gone before us in a world of joy, and to think of them not as lost, but as *found*. They are found in the most beautiful of circumstances, and we do know that, even if we don't always feel it. The souls continue, we know that. But we need to think of them as "continued" and not ended. When we think of our loved ones, we need to focus away from measuring their world with our inadequate tools, and to think of them in their world, finding joy in the simple things they do, finding peace after struggle, and finding ways to send all they have learned back to the earth.

We can perceive those who have traveled the earth before us, and who have struggled like us, as dead, or we can perceive them as living. When we think of the souls, we need to think of them in their surroundings, not ours—otherwise the sky will never be blue for us. Even as we acknowledge our fate and difficult life lessons, we have to go one step further and acknowledge their gain—a new life in a new world that we will also see, when it is our time, and the work on the earth is done. Maybe, in time, we can change the perception of what it is like to have to live under sometimes difficult circumstances on the earth—maybe we can be sad for ourselves but overjoyed at the reward the souls now find for themselves. It takes time, and it takes a willingness to change our perspective, to see from a different lens than we are used to looking. But it can be done because the souls have shown us time and time again that their world is beautiful and worth dreaming about. When we find the peace and serenity to see the end of a long life's journey as a gain for those we know and love, our sky can be any color we imagine it to be, and our long journey will only be a short, bumpy ride until we can put down our tools, pick up our faith, and continue on, just like the souls, to their beautiful world.

I've conducted thousands of sessions, with people from all walks of life and many different circumstances. I've also heard from souls who have encountered many different joys, struggles, accomplishments, problems, differences, and resolutions. Many of the circumstances in people's sessions are the same—the way we live, the way we love, and the way we pass from this existence to the next. But there is a humanity in each of the stories I hear that makes them unique and special, because of the things the souls have learned after having lived, loved, and lost on the earth. The similarities in life are what make us human—but the differences in each of our lives are what make us truly extraordinary.

There is an understanding that many of the souls have come to, once they have made the transition and communicate a full picture of a life on the earth. It's a perspective that none of us on the earth can completely understand or concur with—we have simply not yet finished the portrait of a life on earth. But the souls, from their unique place now in the hereafter, can look back on their lives, and see the finished work. Some of their statements make us think, others make us smile, but a few make us completely rethink our lives and our purpose here. I suppose it's why the souls feel so compelled to keep talking to us.

In sessions, I hear from souls who make their loved ones laugh when they say they are "finally on the vacation they never had" on the earth. It's funny, but it's tragic at the same

time. These were people on the earth who truly struggled—
they worked hard, they raised children, they gave when they
themselves had nothing, and they lived sometimes on the
edge of disaster. Many report having lived in poverty, where
the only thing of value they owned was their faith. Others
lived with the tragic circumstances of loss through violence
or turmoil. Still more gave up the idea of themselves to be
everything to their children, their spouses, their family members, and their community. I listen to the stories told so matter-of-factly that it's astonishing to realize there isn't an
ounce of sarcasm or regret in their voices. Quite the
opposite—these souls say that despite the struggle, the hard
times, and the challenges, they look back on their lives and
the faces of their loved ones here, and they say "It was all so
beautiful." And they *mean* it. Don't get me wrong, it's wonderful to hear—it's just surprising.

But the souls are adamant about it—now that they are out
of the struggle, and now that the struggle has brought them
such joy and peace, they can look back and only see the beautiful moments with their loved ones, the happy times, and
the meaningful journey. And that, they tell me, is more beautiful than they ever imagined.

I started really thinking about that statement, and wondered if that perspective is only relegated to the hereafter.
What I found out startled even me. I read the stories of
Holocaust survivors, who lived through one of the most terrible times in history, and after recounting the awful times,
the pain and the devastation, they seem to have found a

peace within themselves that looks for beauty now, instead of hatred. I have also talked to mothers, especially those who had a difficult pregnancy or painful complications during birth, and though they didn't forget the circumstance, all they know is that they had a beautiful child, and to them, it was worth the pain.

Maybe this is what we are missing when we struggle—maybe we are not looking at life as a means to an end. The souls have told us that each struggle we endure, each heartache we live through, and every reversal of fortune we suffer is a brick in the road that takes us to our reward. Maybe once we receive that reward, the road doesn't seem so awful after all. I hope each of us can take away the message from the souls to see our lives as a work in progress, and to understand that tragedy, loss, suffering, and struggle are a means to an end. If we can understand that, then maybe we can understand our lives a little more, cope a little better, and continue a little lighter than we were before. Maybe it really is *beautiful*.